Photo by Joan Marcus

LA BÊTE

BY DAVID HIRSON

★

DRAMATISTS
PLAY SERVICE
INC.

for

MY PARENTS

and for

STUART OSTROW

LA BÊTE was originally produced on the Broadway stage by Stuart Ostrow and Andrew Lloyd Webber at the Eugene O'Neill Theatre on February 10, 1991. It was directed by Richard Jones; the set and costume designs were by Richard Hudson; the lighting design was by Jennifer Tipton and the sound design was by Peter Fitzgerald. The cast was as follows:

ELOMIRE ....Michael Cumpsty
BEJART...James Greene
VALERE ....Tom McGowan
DORINE ....Johann Carlo
PRINCE CONTI...Dylan Baker
MADELEINE BEJART ....Patricia Kilgarriff
DE BRIE...John Michael Higgins
CATHERINE DE BRIE ....Holly Felton
RENE DU PARC ....William Mesnik
MARQUISE-THERESE DU PARC ....Suzie Plakson
SERVANTS ....Eric Swanson, Cheryl Gaysunas,
Ellen Kohrman, Michael McCormick

In New York, *La Bête* won the John Gassner Award of the Outer Critics Circle, the New York Newsday/Oppenheimer Award, the Marton Prize of the Dramatists Guild, the special Best Play citation in *Best Plays 1990-91,* as well as nominations for five Tony Awards and six Drama Desk Awards including Best Play 1991.

In London, *La Bête* won the 1992 Laurence Olivier Award for Comedy of the Year.

INTRODUCTION

Although it was tempting, in preparing this acting edition of *La Bête*, to provide through amended stage directions a map of the highly stylized and choreographic New York production, I have chosen, with minor exceptions, to present the text without intruding on its original form. My reasons for this are twofold: first, the play was written with an eye towards being as much a pleasure to read as to see, and consequently I felt compelled to preserve the integrity of the initial composition; second, the striking staging at the Eugene O'Neill Theatre, which was designed in a vivid, lopsided world that seized upon the skewed classical/contemporary nature of the piece, and which stressed the tension between purity and excess, rigidity and compromise, style and content, speech and silence, combined elements of vaudeville, dance and pantomime in a way that, for all of its invention, would be fruitless to describe unless I wished that staging alone to be treated as orthodoxy.

Without noting the actual crosses and sometimes balletic movements of the characters, then, I have retained just enough of what appeared on Broadway to give its flavor — a description of Richard Hudson's obtusely angled, "blazing white" set, for example. Any more scrupulous record would seem not only dogmatic but unnecessary since the production itself, as imaginative as it was, always remained extremely faithful to the original text. Hence, those wishing to re-experience it will not be disappointed, nor will future interpreters feel unduly influenced.

It is intriguing to contemplate how other directors will solve, as Richard Jones did so ingeniously, matters of style and choreography in, say, Elomire, Bejart, and Valere's opening sequence, or the first act quartet finale with Dorine, or the Prince's entrance and scene with Elomire, or the Troupe's second act fugue, or "The Parable of Two Boys from Cadiz."

To that end I hope that my stage directions will be observed, as they were in New York, only insofar as they prove useful. And if the Broadway production was visually stunning (Hudson's pristine set, lit with an almost hallucinatory brightness by Jennifer Tipton, becoming gradually more dream-like and defaced in the wake of Valere; costumes ranging from Elomire's austere black-and-white to primary-colored, hybrid 17th/20th-century outfits for the Troupe), the play could just as easily be performed in a completely different design, or in the simplest of styles, with ten actors on a bare stage.

The couplets, of course, require actors who are technically capable, and, under Jones's guidance, each role was played with verbal and physical precision. The Troupe, for instance, moving as one and then exploding in tiny bomb-bursts around the stage, was a glamorous, fastidious group with individually etched personalities: serving as administrators as well as actors, Bejart and Madeleine were portrayed as significantly older and more experienced than the rest, while the Du Parcs, apparently having eclipsed the Bejarts as leading players, sensed the encroachment of the ingenue Catherine and her narcissistic husband De Brie on their own positions. All were viewed as pets by Prince Conti, whose high-handed manner and "iron whim" seemed alternately comic and savage. Dorine — inscrutable, alert, toy-like, silently observing, impatient with the world of language teeming about her — conveyed through gesture and stillness a rich, mysterious interior life. Book-ending the play, she was also its conscience.

While many of these character elements arise naturally from the text, they are to a great extent susceptible to interpretation, and opportunities to vary them, or imagine them differently, are abundant. To encourage experiment I have remained deliberately non-specific about even so fundamental a matter as the characters' ages. Elomire and Valere, like most of the cast, were performed in New York by young actors; it is certainly conceivable that either (or both) could be much older, one of numerous choices whose impact on the production might be interesting and dramatic.

Despite the rigorous demands of the verse, *La Bête* should be enormous fun for actors and audiences alike. It must be played with exuberance and, particularly in the case of Valere, an abandon that is both thrilling and dangerous. Care must be taken, however, to maintain within this comic whirlwind a sense of reality that grows ever more pronounced as the stakes rise. Since no character or position expressed commands an uncomplicated allegiance, the relative weight of the play's arguments will be affected, to an extraordinary degree, by the levels of sympathy, humor and humanity with which each role is invested. Even then, questions about where justice lies are bound to linger, and the play itself is unlikely to yield any simple or definitive answers.

D.T.H.
New York City
November, 1992

CHARACTERS

Members of the Troupe:

ELOMIRE, leader of the troupe
BEJART, his second in command
MADELEINE BEJART, Bejart's sister
DE BRIE
CATHERINE DE BRIE, De Brie's wife
RENE DU PARC
MARQUISE-THERESE DU PARC, Du Parc's wife

VALERE, a troubadour
PRINCE CONTI, patron of the troupe
DORINE, a serving maid

SERVANTS

TIME

1654

PLACE

Prince Conti's estate in Pezenas
Languedoc, France

Note: This play is meant to be performed in an absurdly high comic style, at lightning speed and with rhymes and iambs respected. The costumes are 17th-century bouffe.

Lines spoken simultaneously are indicated by brackets. Where two different conversations are taking place simultaneously they are bracketed and set side by side in two columns.

La Bête is presented in two acts; the action is continuous.

LA BÊTE

ACT ONE

Before the curtain rises, Dorine appears. She surveys the audience and is gone.

The antechamber of the dining room in the actors' cottage: a blazing white environment furnished with a gilt chair and table. Busts of Greek and Roman orators line the cornice. Enter Elomire, storming into the room, followed by Bejart.

ELOMIRE.
    I shall not tolerate another word.
BEJART.
    But Elomire ...
ELOMIRE.
                    Enough, I said ...
BEJART.
                                    I heard!
ELOMIRE.
    THAT COCKATRICE...!
BEJART.
                    Shhhhhhh!
ELOMIRE.   *(Whispering, but viva voce.)*
                            Do it! Throw him out!!
BEJART.
    Good Lord! You whisper ...
ELOMIRE.
                    ... louder than I shout?

So I've been told. Well, good! It's for the better.
(Booming.)
    LET'S HOPE WE'RE OVERHEARD DOWN TO THE
       LETTER...!
BEJART.
    You carry on as if we had a choice!
ELOMIRE.
    We do!
BEJART.
       No!
ELOMIRE.
          Bejart, listen to my voice:
   Our patronage, you say, requires that we
   Add one more player to our company;
   The rationale for this escapes me quite ...
(Bejart begins to protest, but Elomire anticipates.)
   BUT ... knowing that the Court is always right,
   I'm willing to oblige without dispute.
   However, on one point I'm resolute:
   A rash selection simply isn't wise,
(Pointing to the other room.)
   And *that* bombastic ninny I despise!
   Naught could induce me, save a Holy Writ,
   To share the stage with that dull hypocrite!
(Bejart extracts a document from his sleeve.)
   What's that?
BEJART.
       A writ.
ELOMIRE.
       You mock me.
BEJART.
               Au contraire:
*(Elomire, gasping, snatches the document from Bejart's hand and bur-
ies his nose in it.)*
   The Prince, it seems, *adores* Monsieur Valere;
   And though you say he cannot be abided,
   Apparently the matter's been decided...!

ELOMIRE. *(Slumping into a chair, groaning.)*
  O GOD!! I'M GOING TO DIE!!
BEJART.
                                    Well, even so ...

ELOMIRE.
  BUT I *DETEST* VALERE...!!
BEJART.
                          We know, we *know:*
  Repeatedly you've made that understood!
  Withal, the fact remains, our livelihood
  Depends upon a Court decree, and since
  Valere's thought so amusing by the Prince,
  Not only are we bound to cast him ... WORSE!
(Bejart points to a specific clause in the document; Elomire reads, incredulously.)
ELOMIRE.
  "The troupe – might – even – stage his – comic verse"!?
  I'm breaking out in hives! This is obscene!
  What verse? That doggerel that, in between
  Great gulps of *my* Bordeaux, he dared recite? –
  In love with his own voice, the *parasite!*
  "Self-cherishing" is much too mild a phrase
  To give a sense of the coquettish ways
  He forms a sentence, flirting like a girl:
  The tiny cough that says,
(With a tiny cough.)
                          "I've dropped a pearl,"
  The eyelids all a-flutter, and the sniff
  While striking poses with his handkerchief!
  For all of that, he never speaks ... he *spits!*
  I almost drowned in that man's affricates!
  AND HE COMPARES HIMSELF TO SCARAMOUCHE!!
  O, really he's just so grotesquely *louche*
  On all accounts I'd say. Don't you agree?
BEJART. *(Hedging.)*
  Well, what about his generosity
  In showing admiration for your plays...?

ELOMIRE.
    I'd much prefer his censure to his praise!
    Beware of men who laud you to the skies:
    It is *themselves* they mean to lionize!
    Valere finds what he thinks I'd like to hear,
    Then spouts some panegyric that will steer
    The conversation back to his *renown!*
(Imitating Valere.)
    "But have you seen my own, *The Dying Clown?*"
(Ridiculing it.)
    The Dying Clown!
BEJART.
                  I saw it!
ELOMIRE. *(Surprised.)*
                   Really? Where?
BEJART.
    A year ago in Brussels, at a fair.
ELOMIRE.
    Well, was it good?
BEJART.
              I don't remember now;
(But he gradually begins to remember.)
    It was a pantomime ... he had a ...
(Squinting in disbelief at the memory.)
                   ... cow ...
    Dressed up as Anne of Austria!
ELOMIRE.   *(Keening.)*
                 O PLEASE!!
(Slumping to his knees.)
    Look here Bejart: I'm getting on my knees
    To beg the Lord that we be spared this hell:
    "Dear God, we pray ..."
(To Bejart.)
              ... get on your knees as well!
(Bejart ignores him.)
    "DEAR GOD, WE PRAY ..."
(Clutching the pocket of Bejart's coat and pulling him down to his knees.)

                    ... I *mean* it, man, get *down!*
"DEAR GOD, WE PRAY YOU LOOK UPON THIS TOWN
WHERE SEVEN HUMBLE ACTORS MAKE THEIR
    HOME
THANKS TO PRINCE CONTI, BY WHOSE GRACE WE
    ROAM
THE COUNTRYSIDE ITINERANT NO MORE ..."
BEJART.
    Amen.
ELOMIRE.
            Amen? What did you say that for?
BEJART.
    I thought you'd finished.
ELOMIRE.
                        No.
BEJART.   *(Fed up with the histrionics.)*
                        May we get up!?
ELOMIRE.
    "DEAR GOD ..."
BEJART.
                I'm standing ...
ELOMIRE.   *(Reaching out and restraining Bejart.)*
                        "... FROM THY BRIMMING CUP
    OF MERCY LET US DRINK ..."
BEJART.   *(Trying to stand.)*
                        Let go!
ELOMIRE.
                            STAY THERE!
BEJART.
    O, stop it, Elomire! Since when is prayer
    A genuine expression of your creed...?
ELOMIRE.
    When all else fails, goddammit!
BEJART.
                    Damn indeed.
ELOMIRE.
    All right, then: tell me, what do you propose
    Aside from *"pity, that's the way it goes"*?

                        13

How very helpful, what a good solution;
I do applaud your stunning contribution ...
BEJART.
    We simply have no choice!
ELOMIRE.

                           Depressing beast.
BEJART.
    At least I'm honest ...
ELOMIRE.

                        At the *very* least!
Such honesty makes liars of us all:
Just *kneeling* next to you makes me feel small!
Forgive my lack of rectitude, but I,
Immorally, must falsely hope, or die;
Because the merest thought that this *Valere*
Should be forever tangled in my hair
Is so repellent, so abjectly grim,
That, forced to choose between an hour with him
And hanging by my thumbs in Zanzibar ...
BEJART.
    Now don't you think you're taking this too far...?
ELOMIRE.
    ... or writhing in a scalding tub of lye ...
BEJART.
    What would it hurt to give the man a try...?
ELOMIRE.
    ... or rotting in a ditch consumed by lice ...
BEJART.
    In time, I'm sure we'll find he's very nice ...
ELOMIRE.
    ... or wracked with plague, bubonic glands protruding ...
(Enter Valere.)
VALERE.
    GENTLEMEN! I hope I'm not intruding ...
ELOMIRE.   *(Through clenched teeth.)*
    That *voice!* Mon *Dieu!*
VALERE.   *(Seeing Elomire kneeling.)*
                  Good Lord! You're deep in prayer ...

BEJART.

No, no. Come in. Come in, Monsieur Valere.

ELOMIRE.   *(Rolling his eyes at Bejart.)*

Come in...?

VALERE.   Well Heaven Bless Us! *NOW* I see:

It was a sudden burst of piety

That took you from the table, am I right?

(Bejart opens his mouth to speak.)

I'm so relieved! I thought, perhaps, your flight

Was caused by something *I* had said or done ...

(Elomire opens his mouth to speak.)

No, don't explain. GOD BLESS US EVERY ONE!

I, too, am *very pious, most* devout:

I cross myself ... twelve times (or thereabout)

Before I take my morning tea each day!

At lunch I'm up to forty; and I'd say

By nightfall it's ... a staggering amount;

But what a foolish waste of time to count!

(Sniffs and extends handkerchief.)

DEVOTION COMES TO NOTHING IF WE COME

TO SUMMARIZE DEVOTION IN A SUM.

(A slight cough, eyelids flutter, and a self-loving bow.)

A tiny play on words ... doth please you not?

I swear I made it up right on the spot!

I don't know *how* I do it, I just ... do.

These epigrams, they ... come to me as dew

Collects upon a budding daffodil ...

A curse? A blessing? Call it what you will,

It's mine to bear this "genius of the word" –

DID I SAY "GENIUS"?: I think it's absurd

When people call you that, don't you agree?

To us it comes like breath: so naturally.

It seems like sorcery to those below!

I cite that telling phrase from Cicero:

"DE BONUM EST" ... "DIS BONUM EST" ... O, shit ...

Well, anyway, you get the gist of it.

I *do* love Latin. Does it show? It's *true!*

I'm something of a scholar in it, too.

I've read them all (yes, even *I'm* impressed)
From Cicero to ...
(Nervous gulp.)
                              ... you know ... all the rest ...
Whom I could quote in full without abatement:
But I digress ...
ELOMIRE.   *(Under his breath.)*
                    O, what an understatement.
VALERE.
That meal! You must have gone to great expense!
How cruel of me to keep you in suspense!
DID I enjoy it? *WAS* the meal a hit?
(A long pause.)
He turns them slowly, slowly on the spit.
(Thinking he has tortured them, he expounds jubilantly.)
Be at your ease, my friends! I thought the meal
Was excellent ... if not ... you know ... "ideal."
The vinaigrette: a touch acidic, no?
And I prefer less runny *haricots;*
(Singing this line.)
More butter in the velouté next time;
And who, for heaven's sake, told you that lime
Could substitute for lemon in soufflé...?
These tiny points aside, please let me pay
My compliments to all your company,
So generous in breaking bread with me
(Albeit bread that was a wee bit stale);
But I don't want to nitpick. Did I fail
To mention what a charming group they *are?*
Marquise-Therese! *She's* going to be a *star!*
No, no ... I'm *sure* of it! I *know* these things!
So
(Cupping his hands over imaginary breasts.)
      "gifted," and I'm told she even sings!
As for the others, well they tend to be
A little too ...
(With a theatrical flourish.)
                    ... "theatrical" for me ...

But, *darling*, otherwise, words can't *describe*
My deep affection for your little tribe
With whom, I do amuse myself to think,
I shall be privileged to eat and drink
(As we have done this evening) every night!
That is, of course, assuming it's all right.
Am I mistaken? Stop me if I am ...
But it seemed obvious to this old ham
That we had an immediate rapport!
Well-educated people I adore!
It's such a joy to know there's no confusion
When I, whose speech is peppered with allusion,
Refer to facts which few but scholars know:
Arcane, pedantic things like ...
(Nervous gulp.)
                                        ... Cicero ...
And ... other larnèd oddments of that kind
(Indicating himself.)
    (Which, to the truly cultivated mind,
    Are common knowledge more than erudition...)
    But I digress!
(Slapping his own wrist.)
                    O, damn me to perdition!
(To himself.)
    "SHUT UP! SHUT UP! GIVE SOMEONE *ELSE* A
        CHANCE!"
(He covers his mouth with his hands for a beat; then, unable to contain himself for more than a second, he plows on.)
    I've had that said to me all over France ...
    All over Europe, if the truth be told:
    To babble on completely uncontrolled
    Is such a dreadful, *dreadful, DREADFUL* vice!
    Me, I keep my sentences concise
    And to the point ... (well, nine times out of ten):
    Yes, humanly, I falter now and then
    And when I do, naive enthusiasm
    Incites a sort of logorrheic spasm:
    A flood! I mean I don't come up for air!

And even though such episodes are rare
I babble on ... you can't *imagine* how ...
(My God! I'm almost doing it right now!)
NO, NO! I'M ONLY JOKING! NOT TO FEAR!
In fact, I'm far *more* guilty, so I hear,
Of smugly showing that "My lips are sealed ..."
When *I'm* the leading expert in the field!
Of haughtily refusing to debate
When I could easily pontificate!
Instead, I turn away with icy mien
And look ... intimidatingly serene:
As if – you know – the wisdom of the ages
Were silently inscribed upon the pages
Of some majestic tablet in my mind.
But I lay claim to nothing of the kind!
It's others who surround me with this lore;
Myself, I know I'm just a troubadour
With very few accomplishments to boast ...
But, then, I'm more self-critical than most.
You think me *too* self-critical?! Alack,
Ten thousand *more* have launched the same attack!
(Weighing the gem.)
   That's awfully good: "... have launched the same attack!"
   "Ten thousand *more* have launched the same attack!"
(With an oratorical flourish.)
   "YOU THINK ME TOO SELF-CRITICAL?! ALACK,
   TEN THOUSAND *MORE* HAVE LAUNCHED THE SAME
      ATTACK!
(The gem is priceless! Thunderstruck.)
   That's *VERY* close to genius, don't you think?
   If only ...
(Searching the room with his eyes.)
         ... YES! You *HAVE* a quill and ink!
(Rushes to them.)
   I *would* be very grateful ... may I please?
   No time to lose when lightning strikes the trees!
   What did I say again? How did it go?
(As he thinks, a rolling hand gesture to Elomire and Bejart.)

18

(Keep talking ... I'm still listening, you know:
This won't take me a second.) Yes, that's right!
(Scribbling it down.)
"Ten thousand more ..." O, what a pure delight!
One must act quickly on one's inspirations
That they're preserved for future generations;
Behaving otherwise, it seems to me,
Ignores the grave responsibility
Imposed on us (for it's not ours to choose)
By ... what?
(Forms inverted commas with fingers.)
            ... "the lyric gift" ... "the tragic muse" ...
I translate rudely from the words in Greek;
But any tongue sounds coarse when used to speak
Of something so ineffable and high.
Believe me, greater scriveners than I ...
(All right, not "greater," "different": is that fair?)
Have racked their brains and torn out all their hair
In vain pursuit of some linguistic sign
By which mankind might utter the divine.
But what? – "afflatus"? "talent"? – they're too crude,
And I'm a stickler for exactitude
Who chafes at clumsy, earthbound turns of phrase.
True eloquence rings out like godly praise:
There's no mistaking it, it just takes wing.
And, frankly, my own phrase, "THE WONDROUS *THING*,"
Seems loftiest ... more lofty than the Greek!
O! HOW DISGRACEFUL! SLAP ME ON THE CHEEK!
WHAT HUBRIS! WHAT VULGARITY! WHAT NERVE!
NO, SLAP ME! SLAP ME! THAT'S WHAT I DESERVE!
What gall that *I*, the commonest of sods,
Presume to speak more finely than the gods!
Of *course* it may be true, that's not the *point!*
What's ugly is my choosing to anoint
Myself instead of giving you the chance.
No doubt you both must look at me askance
For such a gross, conceited indiscretion:
I pray it won't affect your good impression.

I'm so relieved to get *that* off my chest!
Now that we've put that nagging point to rest
I shall return to my initial theme,
Which is, in short, in fact, to wit, I deem
By way of introduction, SILENCE ALL:
(A pause. Then, with fatuous self-ridicule.)
I HAVEN'T GOT A CLUE! BLANK AS A WALL!
NO, *REALLY,* I'M QUITE SENILE! IT'S NO JOKE!
MY HEAD IS LIKE AN EGG WITHOUT A YOLK!
AND DON'T THINK THIS IS JUST A WAY OF
    STALLING ...
MY MIND HAS *BUCKLED* – ISN'T THAT *APPALLING!?*
THERE'S NOTHING BUT A SPACE BETWEEN MY EARS!
(Change of tone.)
One time I had amnesia in Algiers,
Where everyone is *black* who isn't *white!*
(But that's another tale ...
(With a wink.)
                ... some other night.)
Suffice to say I lost a whole December ...
Or was it August? ... Whoops, I don't remember!
You see how absent-minded I can get!?
(Acting both parts.)
"WHEN DID YOU HAVE AMNESIA?" "I FORGET!"
(He laughs, thrilled.)
Is that not comic genius? I must use it!
I'd better write it down before I lose it!
What did I say ... again ... about forgetting...?
O CHRIST! I've just FORGOTTEN! How UPSETTING!
(Shaking his fist at the sky.)
COME BACK! COME BACK, YOU TANTALIZING GEM!
YOU TEASE! YOU BITCH! YOU FICKLE APOTHEGM!
I GAVE YOU LIFE, AND NOW YOU FLY FROM ME!!
(Apologetically.)
This happens with annoying frequency.
It leads me to exclaim and caterwaul!
Well! Now you've *really* seen me, *warts and all.*
(Suddenly remembering.)

20

ALGERIAN AMNESIA! ...
(Disappointed.)
                              ... no, that's wrong;
O, never mind. More gems will come along;
They always do. Now *where* was I? ... Ah, yes:
You've seen me in a state of stark undress,
My warts exposed, my manner slightly odd:
Well, what would you prefer? Some cheap facade
Of blemishless perfection? Not from ME!
(With a dismissive flick of the wrist.)
GO ELSEWHERE, YE WHO SEEK DISHONESTY;
MY LIFE IS TRUTH, AND TRUTH MY GREATEST
    PASSION!
(Dawning, a revelation.)
Good heavens, both of you are looking ... ashen!
I've been *too* honest, haven't I? But *when?*
WHY CAN'T I LEARN RESTRAINT LIKE OTHER MEN
INSTEAD OF SPILLING EVERYTHING AT ONCE?
(Realizing.)
THE VINAIGRETTE! OF COURSE! I'M SUCH A DUNCE!
HOW COULD I? Please accept my deep regret!
(Putting on his best face.)
Look, I ... *enjoy* ... acidic ... vinaigrette ...
It really makes me ...
(Exploding.)
                    ... GAG!!! ... O!!! THERE, YOU SEE!
I CANNOT LIE! *DAMN* MY INTEGRITY!
I *want* to spare your feelings, yes I do;
But that means saying things that aren't true,
And of my meagre talents, that's not one.
You see, I find that dwelling in the sun
Of honest criticism brings more joy
Than rotting in the darkness of some coy
And sycophantic coterie of slaves.
God! Eloquence comes over me in waves!
Did you hear *that* one? We *all* raised our brows ...
Permit me ... just the ... tiniest of bows,
(He bows.)

I thank you very much, you're far too kind;
As Cicero has famously opined,
"To hear one's peers applaud," ... no! that's not it!
You know the one ... the *famous* one ...
(Exasperated.)

                                    ... *O, shit!*
THE ... ONE ABOUT ... THE NOBLEMEN ...
    COMPETING ...
(After a desperate pause.)
Well, it's so famous it's not worth repeating.
The point is, when a man whom I revere
As highly as the famous ELOMIRE
(Bows to him.)
Should greet my stabs at wit with such approval,
I faint ...
(He slumps into a chair.)
        ... go fetch a cart for my removal!
It's true. No, absolutely, I'm not acting:
The lights grow dim, my pupils are contracting,
My knees go wobbly and my knuckles white,
I'm fading out. Goodnight, sweet world, goodnight ...
(Pause.)
I'm totally unconscious now, I swear.
CAN ANYBODY HEAR ME? ARE YOU THERE?
Perhaps you think I'm being too dramatic;
But, really, I just droop when I'm ecstatic.
(Snaps wide awake.)
What *causes* that? Do either of you know?
A mystic in Gibraltar said I'm low
In some peculiar energy which lies
(For Leos, Capricorns, and Geminis)
Astride the cusp of Saturn's largest moon.
Well, *fine.* But does that tell me *why* I swoon?
Of course it doesn't! What a lot of bunk!
Believe in that stuff and you're really sunk!
Thank God our age has banished superstitions!
(Except for things like sprites and premonitions
Which I think almost certainly are true;

And voodoo dolls and fetishism, too,
Seem eminently credible to me –
And tarot cards and numerology
And cabalistic rituals and such ...)
But that *astrology!* Now there's a *crutch*
That's used by *fools* with *half* a brain, or *none* ...
(Slaps his forehead, and is struck by a vision.)
    WELL, SPEAK OF VISIONS! SOFT! I'M HAVING ONE!
(He describes the vision, eyes half-closed.)
    We're standing in a public square in Ghent
    (I think it's Ghent. It looks like Ghent.
("Let's just say it's Ghent.")

                                    It's *Ghent.*)
    A scarlet banner reads: "A Great Event:
    AUGUSTE VALERE and ELOMIRE Present
    Their Brilliant Spectacle Hailed All Through France ..."
    (And then the title:) "ROMAN ... ," no, "ROMANCE
    OF ...
(Trying to make it out.)
        ... SOMETHING ... SOMETHING ..." Then: "The
        Town of Ghent."
(Impatiently triumphant.)
    (I ... *told* you it was Ghent.) Then there's a tent
    Around which throngs the very cream of Flanders!
(Pauses to savor it.)
    A rousing vision (though it almost panders –
    By promising *such* glory – to my dream
    That like two cloths sewn neatly at the seam
    Our talents might, someday, this world enfold).
    A fancy, merely? Or a truth foretold?
    Won't someone say *which* of the two he thinks it?
    No, no. Don't answer: that would only jinx it,
    And fate's a cranky governess gone gray
    (I coined that phrase in Zürich, by the way,
    When I was EIGHT YEARS OLD! YES, ONLY *EIGHT!*
    Precocious? *Try* PHENOMENAL! *Try* GREAT!
    The envy I provoked just knew no ends.
(Rubbing his hands together.)

Imagine how despised I was by friends!
My tutor fell in love with me of course;
He thought my every word a *tour-de-force!*
I pitied him for doting on me so,
But, then, I *was* a ... *strapping* lad, you know ...
Don't look at me as if I led him on!

(With increasing vehemence, obviously reliving some past tribunal.)
You'd blame a *child* before you'd blame a *don!!??*
I ONLY DID WHAT I WAS TOLD TO DO!!

(Full abreaction.)
   LIES! I NEVER JUMPED HIM! THAT'S NOT TRUE!

(Quickly regaining himself.)
Good heavens! Suddenly it all came back!
So sorry ... seems I wandered off the track ...)
Um ... FATE! ... that's right ... a governess gone gray:
She guides our every movement, and I'd say
Her stewardship goes well beyond the grave;
But if all things are fated, why be brave...?
Or noble? Or industrious? Or fair?

(Schoolmasterish pause, "do I see hands?")
Is that all you can do? Just blankly stare?
Don't tell me this has *never* crossed your mind!
If not, you've waltzed through life completely blind!
Such questions are essential, don't you see?
A solid grounding in philosophy
Is vital to a proper education!
It never entered my imagination
That you could lack this bare necessity ...
(The things I just *assume!* Well, foolish me!)
At risk of sounding pompous or uncouth,
I'd like to list some volumes from my youth
Which might flesh out the ...

(Expressing this as if it were the perfect metaphor, unconscious of the contradiction.)
                   ... bald spots in your learning.
They've made *my* brain more subtle and discerning,
Those great Moroccan-bound and gold-tooled classics,
Which we – the prefects – in our flowing cassocks

Had tucked beneath our arms ...
(Bringing fingers to nose.)
                                        ... I smell them, still!
Indulge me for a moment, if you will.
I recommend you read ... no, I insist ...
An author whom, *remarkably,* you've missed
Since he's the cornerstone of ancient thought
(And – if he's not already – *should* be taught
To every child in every French lycée:)
His name, of course, is ... wait, it *starts* with "A" ...
A *very* famous name, don't help me out;
I *know* it's "A"; it's "A" without a doubt.
It starts with "A." It's "A."
(Slight pause.)
                                        Or *maybe* "D."
(Banishing the ambiguity.)
    No, "A." It's "A." I'm sure it's "A."
(Another ambiguity.)
                                        Or "P."
    It *could* be "P."
(Slight pause.)
                    Or "M."
(Now he's got it!)
                            IT'S "M"! IT'S *"M"!!*
(Crestfallen.)
    O, never mind. It could be all of them.
    Well, this is terrible; I'm just appalled.
    My God! He wrote the famous ... WHAT'S-IT-CALLED,
    COME ON! Don't leave me hanging on a limb!
    You're acting like you've never heard of him,
    And *everybody* has. He's world renowned!
    His writings turned philosophy around
    By altering the then-prevailing view –
    That what is real is really falsely true –
    To what is true is really falsely real ...
(A perplexed squint; then, resuming.)
    Well, *either* way, it's BRILLIANT! Don't you feel?
    And I'm not saying I don't see the *holes;*

Still, it's a stunning glimpse into our souls
No matter *how* you slice it, Q.E.D.
(He won a prize for it ... deservedly.)
But who remembers prizes? It's the *FAME!*
The names of brilliant men like ... what's-his-name ...
Can never be forgotten: *that's* the PRIZE!
Such men live on when everybody dies!
They *laugh* at famine, pestilence and drought:
And isn't that what life is all about?
(Deep breath, as a signal of summation.)
In any case, we've really talked a streak!
Aren't you exhausted? Me? I'm feeling WEAK!!
We've hardly met, and yet you're like my brother
(Playfully sparring.)
The way we banter and play off each other.
We've chatted, chortled, changed our points of view,
We've laughed a little, cried a little, too,
We've had some hills, some valleys and plateaus,
We've traded secrets, quipped in cryptic prose,
We've dropped our guards, we've learned to give a
    damn!
We've proudly cried, "Yes! This is who I am!"
We've said it all, and then ... found more to say;
In short, we've, quote, "just talked the night away."
And surely that's a sign, at least to me,
That this – our partnership – was *meant* to be!
For though we're strangers (in a narrow sense),
In several ways more striking and intense –
Our gift for words, our love of the sublime –
We've known each other since the dawn of time!
(Weighing the gem.)
O, *very* pretty: "... since the dawn of time!"
(With an oratorical flourish.)
"WE'VE KNOWN EACH OTHER SINCE THE DAWN OF
    TIME!"
(Concluding, slapping hands together.)
Well, good! That's all I really planned to *say,*
Except to thank you for a fine soirée

(Treading on eggshells, as if he's saying it for the first time.)
    Spoiled only by acidic vinaigrette,
(Hearing a bell.)
    But then I've said that ... more than once, I'll bet!
    My head is in the clouds: pay no attention!
    It's off in some ethereal dimension
    Where worldly thoughts not instantly deleted
    Are roundly and mechanically repeated
    As if to pacify the earth below.
    How galling it must be for you to know
    That even as we speak, within my mind
    I might be off in some place more refined –
    That even though I'm present by convention,
    You may not really have my full attention ...
    I don't mean *you specifically,* dear friend!
    Good heavens! Would I dare to condescend
    To someone as illustrious as you!?
    I mean, of course, the *common* people who
    Would stoop to kiss my hem they so adore me:
    Forgive them, Lord! They know not how they bore me
    With idle chatter of their simple ways!
    I'm sorry, but my eyes begin to glaze
    And it's a chore to keep myself awake
    When someone's telling me about a rake
    Or if his soil will yield a healthy grape.
    I smile and nod, but silently escape
    To knowledgable regions in my dome
    More crowded than a Roman hippodrome!
    I have, for instance (and it's not a fluke)
    Verbatim recall of the Pentateuch!
    Incredible? It's *true!* Just watch and see:
    From Genesis to Deuteronomy
    I now recite the Scriptures, LEARNED BY HEART!!:
    "IN THE BEGINNING ..."
(Squinting, trying to remember more.)
                       ... yes, well that's the start;
(Moving right along.)
    It goes on just like that till Moses dies.

A superhuman task to memorize?
Not really. It's so *good,* it rather *stuck* ...
(To himself.)
But I digress! SHUT UP YOU STUPID CLUCK,
AND LET *THESE* GENTLE PEOPLE TALK A MITE!
(Dramatically extending handkerchief.)
Look, gag me with this handkerchief, all right?
I know that sounds extreme, and I'm a stranger,
But trust me: you are in the gravest danger!
For my digressions (left unchecked) can reach
The vast proportions of a major speech;
And you have no *idea* how close I am
To just that sort of frantic dithyramb!
So why not spare yourselves a living hell
And gag me!
 (He touches the handkerchief to his mouth, snapping it away long enough to finish the line; he continues to do so, the handkerchief hovering.)
                GAG ME! TIE ME UP, AS WELL!
RESTRAIN ME! DISCIPLINE ME! HOLD ME BACK!
HUMILIATE ME! GIVE THE WHIP A CRACK!
DISGRACE ME: MAKE ME BARK AND WEAR A DRESS
AND LICK THE FILTHY FLOOR WHEN I DIGRESS!
But in the meantime, gagged I *should* remain:
It's better that way, no? It's such a sane
And healthy way to curb my domination.
I find it a *complete* abomination
(No matter how distinguished one might be)
When every word is "ME ME ME ME ME."
ME, I'm far too interested in others;
And frankly, friends, were I to have my "druthers"
I'd utter not a peep for weeks untold,
Preferring to ... absorb the manifold
Of human speech: the "babel" of the masses.
Just stop and *listen* to the lower classes!
You'll have an education when you're done
That rivals twenty years at the Sorbonne!
For in their mindless grunts, the bourgeoisie

Express what I call "wise stupidity."
But no one listens anymore, I fear,
And when I die, so too will disappear
That subtle art, whose practice now grows faint.
And I'm not saying I'm some stained-glass saint
Who *always* listens. Always? No, indeed!
My God! I'm human! Cut me and I bleed!
It's simply that, as far as mortals go,
I'm sensitive (and some say too much so)
To any nuance in a conversation
Which *might, PERHAPS,* suggest my domination.
Thus, in mid-sentence often I just cease ...
(Despite the countless times I've held my peace
When, in the end, I might as well have chattered
Since only *I* said anything that mattered!
I know that sounds repulsive, but it's true.)
The point is, this is something that I do
Against all logic; so don't be distraught
If, in the middle of a brilliant thought,
I stop like this ...
(Freezes; continues.)
                    ... depriving you of more;
Or if, commanding reverence from the floor
For awesome skills debating pro *or* con,
I simply stop like this ...
(Freezes; continues.)
                         ... and don't go on!
A trifle strange, *n'est-ce pas?* But, if you please,
Ask any of my many devotees:
They'll tell you that this quirk (at first appearing)
In time becomes ...
(Freezes; continues.)
                    ... incredibly endearing!
(Guffaw of self-delight.)
To *me* it seems *obnoxious,* heaven knows;
But most say it's a charming trait that grows
More sweet with each encounter! TELL ME WHY!
I just don't see it ... but: then who am I?

At any rate, THE GAG! OF COURSE! Let me:
Observe with what profound simplicity
It does the job. I think you'll be surprised.
VOILÀ!
(He stuffs the gag into his mouth, then continues, half-audibly.)
                    Now isn't this more civilized!
I'm silenced and I think we're *all* relieved!
We've nipped me in the bud, and thus retrieved
The limelight for our precious Elomire.
Speak on, my friend! This player longs to hear
If in posterity you'll deign to share
Your splendid name with one AUGUSTE VALERE!
Please answer lest I talk you both to death:
(Removes the gag.)
I wait on your reply with bated breath.
*(Valere stuffs the gag back into his mouth, assumes a theatrical pose
and: blackout. Lights up quickly. Silence. A moment passes. Elomire
and Bejart circle the frozen Valere, reaching out to touch him and
jerking their fingers back. Finally, Elomire faces him directly.)*
BEJART.

                                        Do you think he's ill?

ELOMIRE.
    O, yes.
BEJART.
            Then we should ...
ELOMIRE.
                            No, Bejart! Be still!
Let's use this brief caesura while we can!
MONSIEUR VALERE: You seem to be a man
In love with words, a *true* aficionado ...
VALERE.
    I'm *that* transparent!?
ELOMIRE.
                        Yes ...
VALERE.
                        But it's bravado!
Don't let my gift – "the silver tongue" – deceive you;

I'm *really* foolish ...

BEJART.

                              Yes, we both believe you. ⎫

ELOMIRE.

                              Yes, we both believe you. ⎭

VALERE.   *(Bowing.)*

  You're gentle ...

ELOMIRE.

                              Nonetheless it's very clear

  That language is a thing which you hold dear ...

VALERE.

  Too mild! Too mild! It's more than dear to me!

  I liken syntax to morality –

  Its laws inviolate in such a way

  That damned is he who dares to disobey!

  Diction, like aesthetics, is more free:

  It's where we show our creativity

  By choosing metaphors and ways of speech –

  I'd say "the shell-crushed strand"; you'd say "the
      beach."

  Semantics is like ... (hang on ... let me see ...

  I've *used* aesthetics and morality ...)

  Semantics is like ... SWIMMING! ... (no, that's bad!

  O, DAMMIT! DAMMIT! DAMN, I thought I had

  A brilliant speech developing! *DOMMAGE!*)

  Well ... back to our exciting persiflage ...

(Deep inhale, eyes cross.)

  Where were we...?

ELOMIRE.

                    Language.

VALERE.

                              Gasp! My greatest passion!

ELOMIRE.

  But ...

VALERE.

            Please no buts! It *can't* go out of fashion!

  Verbobos are as ancient as the birds!

ELOMIRE.
Verbobos?
VALERE.
Yes.
ELOMIRE.
What's that?
VALERE.
My word for "words."
ELOMIRE.
Your word for "words"?
VALERE.
Correct.
ELOMIRE.
Why?
VALERE.
"Words" sounds dreary;
"VERBOBOS." I prefer it. It's more ... cheery!
"VERBOBOS"! Say it! COME ON *EVERYONE!*
BEJART.
Verbobos.
ELOMIRE.   *(Wheeling on Bejart.)*
Shut up.
VALERE.
THERE! YOU SEE!? IT'S FUN!!
ELOMIRE.
You make up words?
VALERE.
Why, yes. Is it a crime?
ELOMIRE.
You can't just do that ...
VALERE.
Do it *all the time!*
For instance ...
(Searching the room with his eyes.)
... "CHAIR": now there's a pallid noun!
Well, I refuse to say it sitting down!
"FRANCESCA" is the word I use instead;
Or "TABLE": there's a word that's good as dead!

One might say "escritoire" but that's too frilly,
And "desk-like thing" sounds just a little silly,
So I say *"CARABOOMBA"* ... which, you see,
Endows the "TABLE" with nobility.

(Valere, demonstrating, takes the quill and scrawls the words on the wall, as if writing on a blackboard; Elomire and Bejart stare in shock and disbelief.)

"FRANCESCA CARABOOMBA": most expressive!
It really is amazingly impressive
How clearly the *verbobos* I invent
Outshine (and do not *simply* supplement)
The ancient phonemes of our mother tongue.
But that's a *"flecund"* point which you must *"drung"* ...

ELOMIRE.
Monsieur Valere: I *hate* to interrupt ...

VALERE.
I know the feeling ...

ELOMIRE.
But I'll be abrupt,
And speak to you directly if I can:
You know as well as I that you're a man
Whose talents and abilities would be
Much better served in some ... fraternity ...

BEJART.
A guild, perhaps ...

ELOMIRE.
Precisely! In some GUILD,
Where you would feel more happy and fulfilled
Than you could ever feel by staying here ...

(Valere's attention has wandered to Bejart's humpback, which he notices for the first time.)

VALERE.   *(To Bejart.)*
Is that a humpback?

BEJART.
Yes.

VALERE.
O DEAR DEAR DEAR!
How *deeply* nauseating! How *unsightly!*

There's just no way of putting this politely!
(Speaking loudly to Bejart as if he were deaf.)
　　YOU MAKE ME ILL; I'M SURE YOU UNDER-
　　　　STAND!
(Examining the hump.)
　　Perhaps if I could ... touch it with my hand –
　　You know – for luck ...
(As Valere reaches out to touch the hump, Bejart pulls away in disgust.)
　　　　　　　　　　　　 ... all right then, BE that way!
　　MY GOD! We're all so *sensitive* today!
ELOMIRE.
　　DID YOU JUST HEAR ME?
VALERE.
　　　　　　　　　　　　　　 HOW WAS *I* TO KNOW!??
　　At dinner, hunched above his escargots
　　He seemed ill-mannered merely, not contorted;
　　But clearly my impression was distorted ...
BEJART.
　　How dare you!
VALERE.
　　　　　　　　　 No, I think it's *good!* I *DO!*
(Trying to envision a potential hump on the other side.)
　　Too bad there can't be even *more* of you!
　　I'm thrown, that's all; but isn't that expected?
　　I've seen you act, but never once detected
　　Until this moment, standing in this room,
　　That you were ... *ripped untimely from the womb!*
　　Now *why* is that?
BEJART.
　　　　　　　　　　 I don't know *what* to say ...
VALERE.　　*(Wheeling on Elomire, a revelation.)*
　　YOU WRITE A HUMPBACK INTO EVERY PLAY!
ELOMIRE.
　　Monsieur Valere...!
VALERE.
　　　　　　　　　 Of course! That's it! It's *true!*
(Turning to Bejart.)

34

The reason that I'd never noticed you
Were cruelly maimed is that you play the roles
Of humpbacked beggars, philistines and trolls
Which Elomire specifically designed
With your misshapen body in his mind!

BEJART.
You're MAD...!

VALERE.
You mean I'm RIGHT...!

BEJART.
I mean you're MAD...!

VALERE.
You mean I'm *RIGHT!!*

BEJART.
You're *MAD!!*

VALERE.
I'm *RIGHT!!*

ELOMIRE.
I'VE HAD
ENOUGH! ENOUGH! ENOUGH OF THIS...!

VALERE.
ME, TOO!

(Pause.)
Enough of what, exactly, though...?

ELOMIRE.
... of YOU!!

VALERE.
I'm sorry?

ELOMIRE.
YOU! AND LET THERE BE NO DOUBT!

VALERE.
I hear you, darling, you don't have to shout ...

ELOMIRE.
O, yes I do! And let me tell you why:
I've listened to you speak ... no, "speechify"
For what seems like a century in hell:
Enough, I think, to know you all too well –
Or well enough to wish I didn't know you...!

VALERE.
You lost me there ...
ELOMIRE.

O, yes? Then let me show you
In very *basic* language if I may ...
BEJART.
Don't be a fool ...
ELOMIRE.

I'M GOING TO HAVE MY SAY!
BEJART.
THE WRIT!
ELOMIRE.

I KNOW!
BEJART.

WELL IF YOU KNOW, DESIST!!
VALERE.
(Good heavens! Is there something that I missed?)
BEJART.
OUR HANDS ARE TIED!!
ELOMIRE.

NOT MINE!! NOT ANY-
MORE!!
BEJART.
THEN PICK HIM UP AND THROW HIM OUT THE
DOOR!!
ELOMIRE.
I PLAN TO!!
BEJART.

IF THAT'S SO WE'RE FINISHED HERE!!
Prince Conti's writ is absolutely clear,
And I, for one, am not, like you, prepared
To risk what we've achieved ...
ELOMIRE.

Because you're *scared!*
BEJART.
Because I'm *CAUTIOUS!*
ELOMIRE.

God! That's even WORSE!

VALERE.

(It's like a drama – only not in verse ...)

BEJART.

What shame is there in safety? What disgrace?
In middle age are you prepared to face
What we, the decade past, have struggled through?
And I'm not thinking just of me and you –
Marquise-Therese ...

VALERE.

(Now there's a "gifted" wench!)

BEJART.

... De Brie, and Catherine, whom you would wrench
Away from all the comforts of this "home" –
Again to sleep in haylofts and to roam
From burg to parish living hand-to-mouth!
Remember how they booed us in the south?

VALERE.

(The *south*? The *SOUTH*? Why in the *SOUTH* they *cheer*
   me!)

BEJART.

I just don't think it's worth it, do you hear me?

VALERE.

(And I don't mean applause, I mean *OVATIONS...*!)

BEJART.

Why jeopardize this best of situations
For lack of patience? Life is compromise!
We learn to live with that which we despise
In cases where the benefits outweigh
Whatever penance we are forced to pay.
Forbearance is a virtue ...

ELOMIRE.

In a *saint!*

But men who would endure without complaint
An insult to preserve some meagre gain
Deserve not only pity but disdain.

VALERE.

(I side with *him!*)

BEJART.

                  That's very well to *say,*
But who on earth can ever live that way?
We're hypocritical, by definition ...

VALERE.

    (I think he's swaying me to *his* position ...)

BEJART.

    We're all more guilty than we'd dare admit
Of daily bending principles to fit
Ignoble appetites, which I contend
Is nobler than deciding *not* to bend
One's principles despite the likelihood
That they may finally do more harm than good.

VALERE.

    (Well, that's what *I* would say ...)

ELOMIRE.

                            I disagree!
To suffer for one's principles, to me
Seems nobler than to prosper from their lack.

VALERE.

    (That's true. Good point ...)

BEJART.

                   It's not so white and black!
I'm arguing for something in between ...

VALERE.

    (He's right, you know ...)

ELOMIRE.

               By which, of course, you mean
You advocate a plan that when applied
Insures that everyone's dissatisfied.

VALERE.

    (O, that's *so* true. I'm on *your* side again!)

ELOMIRE.

    Our lives are governed by such *foolish* men!
And we're to blame because, misguidedly,
We hold to the belief that it would be
More difficult to keep a fool at bay
Than simply just to ... let him have his way.

At first this seems a harmless compromise,
But hot air has the tendency to rise
Until it finally overwhelms your life!
That's when a fool will *really* twist the knife –
When he gets power! And he always does!
Then grit your teeth and swallow hard because
He'll mock you every day with your mistake
Of underestimating what a snake
A fool can be if given half a chance!
He'll treat you like the footman at a dance
And revel, with Mephistophelean glee,
In how his presence shall, eternally,
Evoke, with sharp refrains of ridicule,
The cutting truth that *you've been* made the fool!!
But wait! – you're really *more* the fool than he,
Because no simple fool could ever be
So foolish to neglect the simple rule
That only fools will tolerate a fool!
Tonight was just a warning – DID YOU HEAR HIM!!??
And sitting silently because we fear him
Is no solution in the grander scheme.
He won't just disappear like some bad dream:
We're going to have to face this matter squarely!

BEJART.
I really think you're acting most unfairly!

ELOMIRE.
Unfairly? How?

BEJART.
    I'm *so* embarrassed!

ELOMIRE.
         Why?

Because of *me*?

BEJART.
    You know as well as I!

ELOMIRE.
You mean because I'm showing him our hand?
I promise you, he doesn't understand.
They never do! The foolish aren't that wise!

BEJART.   *(He pivots to Valere.)*
    Monsieur Valere: I must apologize
    For this disgraceful spectacle ...
ELOMIRE.

                                        ... disgrace!?

BEJART.
    AND DAMAGING!
ELOMIRE.

                        But how is that the case?
    I promise you our words went unattended!
    Valere, I ask you: have you been offended
    By anything I've said?
VALERE.

                        Me? Heavens, no!
    I'm on *your* side in this, I *told* you so!
    (Half taking Elomire aside, speaking in a stage whisper.)
        (You're such a better speaker than *that* chap!
    (Indicating Bejart's humpback with a wink.)
    But then ... of course ... he's got a handicap.)
    No, why on earth should I have felt abused!!??
    I'm *flattered* by that M-word that you used!
    "MERISTORELEAN" was it...?
ELOMIRE.   *(To Bejart.)*

                        There, you see?

VALERE.
    I'm touched you'd think it might apply to *me!*
    "He's so MERISTO –" what? ...
ELOMIRE.

                            Mephistophelean.

VALERE.
    MERISTORELEAN! YES! MERISTORELEAN!
    "He's so *MERISTORELEAN!*" ...
ELOMIRE.   *(To Bejart.)*

                        There, you see?
    Completely blinded by his vanity.
    *(Cross-talk as Valere poses, trying on the word "Meristorelean," and
    Elomire continues to lecture to Bejart. We should hear Elomire clearly,
    Valere as background.)*

ELOMIRE.

VALERE.

ELOMIRE.	VALERE.
And I assure you that it wouldn't matter	He's so MERISTORELEAN when he walks!
If I just served it to him on a platter!	He's so MERISTORELEAN when he talks!
The bluntest terms would float beyond his ken;	He's so MERISTORELEAN when he prays!
I'm telling you: I *know* these kind of men!	I envy his MERISTORELEAN ways!
You don't believe me? Watch! I'll demonstrate:	MERISTORELEAN! *So* MERISTORELEAN!
Monsieur Valere: permit me to restate ...	MERISTORELEAN! *So* MERISTORELEAN! ...

ELOMIRE.

MONSIEUR VALERE! I need your full attention!
I wonder: might I have the chance to mention
In more specific terms (if that's all right)
My own impressions of our chat tonight?

VALERE.

O, *be* specific! YES! *Please* do! I'm *rapt!*

ELOMIRE.

Well, good...!

BEJART. *(To Elomire.)*

You know, you really should be slapped!

VALERE.

But let me sit in this

VALERE.

FRANCESCA.

ELOMIRE.

FRANCESCA.

VALERE.

Wait!

O, good idea! Now I can concentrate!
(He looks ostentatiously riveted.)

ELOMIRE.

I'm glad you're concentrating. Listen closely:

41

You've said a lot tonight and said it grossly.
In fact ... I've been appalled by every word!
I find your views on life and art absurd,
And yet one hardly notices above
The mountain of your towering self-love!
Your ignorance is even more colossal –
Your brain is like some prehistoric fossil:
It must have died ten thousand years ago!
But on and on and on and on you go
As if you were the fount of human learning!
And selfishly, contemptuously spurning
The moves that others make to interject,
You act as if you're one of "the elect"
Whom God appoints like Jesus Christ our Savior!
It really is contemptible behavior
Whose only saving grace (if one there be)
Is in the unintended comedy
Arising from your weightiest pronouncements!
You seem to feel you have to make announcements
Instead of speaking in a normal tone;
But by your orotund and overblown
And hectoringly pompous presentation,
You simply magnify the desolation,
The vast aridity within your soul!
In short, I think you're just a gaping hole –
A talentless, obnoxious pile of goo!
I don't want anything to do with you!
I can't imagine anyone who would!
And if it makes me better understood
To summarize in thirty words or less,
I'd say you have the power to depress
With every single syllable you speak,
With every monologue that takes a week,
And every self-adoring witticism! ...
VALERE.
Well, do you mean this as a *criticism?*
ELOMIRE.   (*Throws up his hands; to Bejart.*)
I rest my case.

VALERE.
>
> And when you say "depress"
> Do you mean *bad* "depress" or *good* "depress"?
> And overblown's defined exactly *how?*

ELOMIRE.

> There, Bejart? Do you believe me *now?*

VALERE.

> Would it be overreaching to request
> That you write down, so that I might digest
> At greater length, and also at my leisure,
> The comments you just made, which I shall treasure!

BEJART.

> I'm flabbergasted! I don't understand!
> I've never heard a more perverse demand!
> Why would you want them written down?

VALERE.

> To read them.

BEJART.

> Well, yes. Of course. But why?

VALERE.

> I'm going to need them.

BEJART.

> But *why?*

VALERE.

> Because I'm anxious to *improve!*
> Is that so strange, my wanting to remove
> The flaws from my persona? Surely not!
> I loathe a blemish! I despise a spot!
> Perfection is the goal towards which I strive
> (For me, that's what it means to be alive)
> And, hence, I'm grateful for a shrewd critique:
> It keeps my talent honest, so to speak!
> We of the theatre share that common view –
> The criticisms of the things we do
> Inspire our interest, not our hurt or rage:
> We know it's part of "being on the stage"
> To have oneself assessed at every turn,
> And thus we show a willingness to learn

From judgments which might wound another man.
I much prefer to any drooling fan
A critic who will SLICE me into parts!
GOD *LOVE* THE CRITICS! *BLESS* THEIR PICKY HEARTS!
Precisely, and in no uncertain terms,
They halve the apple, showing us our worms.
(Staggering slightly.)
(My God, that was a *brilliant* illustration!)
(Regaining himself.)
Don't get me wrong: to hear some dissertation
On all one's failings gives a twinge of course:
It smarts when someone knocks you off your horse –
That's true for anybody I should think!
But climbing on again in half a wink
And knowing that you're better for the spill
Instructs us that it's love and not ill-will
That motivates a critical assault.
You've *honored* me tonight by finding fault!
Which doesn't mean I don't feel vaguely crushed ...
I *do!* I'm *bruised!* But who would not have blushed
To hear himself discussed so centrally?
"My God," I thought, "Are they denouncing *me*,
These men of such *distinction* and *renown!*?
How thrilling *I'm* the one they're tearing down!!
What joy that Elomire, whom people say
Is destined to become the next Corneille,
Should slander *me* in such a public forum!"
And, by the way, it isn't just decorum
Which prompts me to express my awe of you;
Your plays, I think, show genius, and a few
(Like *Mandarin*) I've seen five times or more.
Now there's a play that really made me roar!
I haven't laughed so hard in years and years!
ELOMIRE.
It was a tragedy.
VALERE.
But through my *tears*
The laughter seemed more painful ... (O MY GOD!

WELL, OPEN MOUTH, INSERT THY FOOT, YOU
    CLOD!
COULD THAT HAVE BEEN MORE AWKWARD?
    SURELY NOT!
(Fanning himself.)
    I'M SO EMBARRASSED! WHEW! MY FACE IS HOT!)
Forgive me, Elomire. What can I say?
I'm sure it was a very solemn play.
But why, then, did *I* find it such a hoot?
The crippled peasant boy who played the flute:
Hysterical! I mean I was delirious!
I must have nodded off when it got serious!
Are you quite sure it was a tragedy?
(Bejart intervenes sternly, extending his hand to Valere.)
BEJART.
    It's time to say goodnight, it seems to me.
ELOMIRE.
    No no, Bejart: It's time to say good*bye!*
BEJART.
    That's not an option!
ELOMIRE.
                        Why?
BEJART.
                            I've *told* you why!
(Enter Dorine, the serving maid. She speaks in a high-pitched falsetto.)
ELOMIRE.
    Then ...
DORINE.
            BLUE!
BEJART.
                Hello?
ELOMIRE.
                    Who's there?
VALERE.
                                Your maid.
ELOMIRE.
                                        Ah, yes!

Come in, Dorine.
(*She descends the step.*)
                    Be careful with your dress.
DORINE.
  BLUE!
ELOMIRE.
          Good girl. Now what's the matter, dear?
DORINE.
  BLUE!
ELOMIRE.
          Yes, blue; blue *what*?
DORINE.

                              BLUE!!
ELOMIRE.

                        "Blue" is clear;
  Blue what, though!?
DORINE.
          BLUE!!
ELOMIRE.
                        Blue *what!*? Blue *what!*?
(*He sighs deeply, as if overwhelmed by the tedium of having to go
through something which he has endured many times before; rolling
his eyes.*)

                              Blue ... SKIES?
(*Dorine shakes her head no.*)
  Blue ... MOON?
(*Dorine shakes her head no.*)
          Blue ... CHEESE?
(*Dorine shakes her head no.*)
VALERE.   (*To Bejart.*)
                    What's going on!?
ELOMIRE.

                              Blue ... EYES?
(*Dorine shakes her head no.*)
VALERE.   (*To Bejart.*)
  Is this some sort of guessing game she plays?
BEJART.
  No, no. It's just an adolescent phase ...

46

ELOMIRE.
   Blue ... *WHAT*, DORINE!? This drives me up the wall!!
(He pinches the bridge of his nose and continues to search his mind in irritation.)
VALERE.   *(To Bejart.)*
   What sort of phase?
BEJART.
                                    She never speaks at all
   Except in monosyllables like ...
DORINE.
                                    BLUE!!
BEJART.
   ... or words which rhyme to that effect like "two"
   Or "do" or "shoe": don't ask me to explain;
   These adolescent phases are insane!
VALERE.
   She only speaks in words which rhyme with "do"?
BEJART.
   That's right.
VALERE.   *(Gravely.)*
                     What are our children coming to?
(Back to Bejart.)
   How long has this been going on?
BEJART.
                                            For weeks!
VALERE.
   But can you understand her when she speaks?
BEJART.
   Well, yes and no: it takes some time, you see.
(Dorine indicates her left wrist as if playing a game of charades.)
ELOMIRE.
   Blue ... what? Blue what? Blue WRIST!?
BEJART.
                                            Eventually
   She gets her point across ...
ELOMIRE.
                              Blue WRIST!? Blue ...
(Dorine slashes her left wrist with her right hand.)

DORINE.   *(Emphatically.)*

                                                                  BLUE!!

VALERE.
    Now what's she doing?
BEJART.

                            Giving us a clue.
(Dorine is slashing at her wrist emphatically.)
ELOMIRE.
    You're slashing at your wrist.
(Dorine nods vigorously.)

                            Blue SLASH?
*(Dorine shakes her head no, impatiently trying to get someone to say
"blood.")*

                                        Blue ... CUT!?
(Dorine continues her miming.)
    O, I don't know, Dorine! Blue WHAT!? Blue WHAT!?
*(Dorine mimes an act of hara-kiri, at the end of which her internal
organs figuratively spill out onto the floor.)*
VALERE.
    Blue blood.
*(Dorine snaps her fingers and points to Valere, giving an "on the
nose": he got it!)*
ELOMIRE.

                        Blue *blood?*
*(She nods vigorously, still pointing at Valere, jumping up and
down.)*

                            That's it? You mean he's right?
*(More of the same from Dorine; Valere throws up his arms victori-
ously, as if acknowledging the adulation of a large crowd.)*
VALERE.
    Well! This is turning out to be my night!
    I wasn't even trying and I won
    (Which makes the victory that much more fun!!).
ELOMIRE.
    But what does "blue blood" signify?
BEJART.

                                    To me
    It would imply the aristocracy ...

ELOMIRE.
Or royalty, perhaps ...
(Dorine points excitedly.)
BEJART.

Ah, yes! That's true!
(Dorine is pointing, nodding; "royalty" is correct! Cross-talk as Valere presses on in his own direction.)
ELOMIRE.
That's *it*, Dorine? That's what you meant by BLUE?? ⎫
DORINE.

BLUE!! ⎪

⎬

VALERE.
The answer came to me out of the   BLUE!! ⎭
VALERE.
I realize now I should have warned you, though,
That I'm an ace as far as word games go ...
ELOMIRE.   *(Nailing it down.)*
So "royalty," Dorine, would be correct?
(Dorine nods vigorously.)
VALERE.
One Easter, while performing near Utrecht
VALERE.
(A dreary, dreary backwash of a town) ... ⎫

⎬

ELOMIRE.   *(To Bejart.)*
It's "royalty": at least we've nailed *that* down ... ⎭
BEJART.
But what's significant about the crown?
VALERE.
... I fell into a local Flemish game ...
ELOMIRE.
Indeed, Dorine!
VALERE.

... "BAMBOOZLE" was its name ...
ELOMIRE.
Just why is "royalty" so apropos?
VALERE.
... Whose rules – MY GOD! – I didn't even know ...

49

BEJART.
Speak up my girl!
VALERE.

... But somehow I kept winning!

DORINE.
NEW!
BEJART.
New WHAT?
ELOMIRE.

New *WHAT*?

DORINE.

NEW!

ELOMIRE.

New ... BEGINNING!?

(Shaking her head no, Dorine cradles an imaginary baby in her arms; and Valere responds to Elomire as if "BEGINNING" referred to the story that he has been telling.)
VALERE.
BEGINNING? ... *Yes:* I'd never played before!
ELOMIRE.   *(Responding to Dorine's pantomime.)*
New ... BORN??
(Dorine shakes her head no.)
VALERE.

That's why, when tallying the score,

VALERE:	BEJART.
I gasped and turned a thousand shades of red	New CHILD?? New INFANT? What else could it be??
To find the victor's garland on my head ...	ELOMIRE. Dorine, you're really irritating me!!

ELOMIRE.   *(Continuing; to Bejart.)*
She tries my patience!
VALERE.

... *And* I won a prize...!!

ELOMIRE.
I'm fed up with these single-word replies!!

VALERE.
    ... A silver goblet...!!
DORINE.   *(Still cradling an imaginary baby.)*
                    NEW!!
ELOMIRE.

                        Enough, Dorine!!
    Now act your age and tell me what you mean!!
BEJART.
    New BABY, maybe?
(Dorine shakes her head no.)
VALERE.

                    ... no no no, it's *pewter* ...

ELOMIRE.
    If she goes on like this I'm going to shoot her!
BEJART.
    New BIRTH?
(Dorine shakes her head no.)
VALERE.

                    ... or ...

BEJART.
                    New ARRIVAL?
*(Dorine excitedly nods, jumps up and down and gives the "on the
nose" signal.)*
VALERE.

                            ... is it copper...?

BEJART.
    ARRIVAL?? New *ARRIVAL*??
(Dorine is nodding vigorously.)
ELOMIRE.

                    Can't we stop her?

VALERE.
    ... Or is it brass...?
BEJART.
                    No need to, Elomire:
    The answer's "new ARRIVAL," did you hear?
VALERE.
    ... In any case, I keep it on display ...

ELOMIRE.
That's *it*, Dorine? That's what you meant to say?
(*Dorine nods vigorously.*)
VALERE.
... and clutch it to my breast when I'm in bed ...
(*Bejart is squinting, trying to piece it together.*)
BEJART.
Dorine, repeat the first word that you said!
VALERE.
... which isn't ...
DORINE.
                    BLUE!
BEJART.
                              Which means
VALERE.
                                        ... because I'm proud ...
BEJART.
That royalty is
DORINE.
                    NEW!
VALERE.
                              ... it's that I vowed
To guard that chalice with my life and limb!
BEJART.   (*A solution dawning.*)
My God! Of course! It must refer to him!
ELOMIRE.
My God of course it must refer to *whom?*
VALERE.
... One time I had it stolen from my room ...
BEJART.
PRINCE CONTI'S HERE!
ELOMIRE.
                    PRINCE *CONTI?*
DORINE.
                                        TRUE!!
VALERE.
                                             ... In shock ...

52

ELOMIRE.
  But why?
BEJART.
            Because
VALERE.
                ... I checked behind the clock ...
BEJART.   *(Emphasizing the words as if to say, "It's obvious.")*
  A *new* ARRIVAL! Blue for *ROYALTY!*
VALERE.
  ... And lo! ...
ELOMIRE.
            Good heavens!
DORINE.
                    TRUE!!
ELOMIRE.
                        You're right!
VALERE.
                            ... I see
  My trophy wedged against the wall! ...
ELOMIRE.
                        DORINE!
  PRINCE CONTI'S HERE RIGHT NOW? *THAT'S* WHAT
      YOU MEAN!?
(Dorine nods vigorously.)
VALERE.
  ... It must have slipped ...
ELOMIRE.
                WELL SEND HIM IN!
VALERE.
                            ... My cup
  Had, therefore, *not* been stolen ...
ELOMIRE.
                HURRY UP!
VALERE.
  ... And I was *so* relieved at simply knowing
  That it was mine again ...
(Seeing Dorine leaving.)
                WAIT! WHERE'S SHE GOING?

(She turns around.)
   Before you leave ... one question please Dorine:
   How old are you, dear?
DORINE.

                        TWO!

BEJART.   *(Translating.)*

                        She's seventeen.

ELOMIRE.
   NOW RUN ALONG!
(Exit Dorine.)
VALERE.

                        Then why did she say "two"?

BEJART.
   I thought I just explained that quirk to you.
VALERE.
   Ah, yes! Indeed! The adolescent phase!
   I must admit, I felt my eyebrows raise
   When she said two years old! I was astounded!
   I thought, "My God! Just 'two,' and so well ...
(Cupping his hands over his chest like breasts.)

                        ... rounded!"

ELOMIRE.   *(To Bejart, reproving.)*
   You didn't tell me he was coming here!
BEJART.
   Because I didn't know it, Elomire:
   They handed me this writ, that's all I knew!
VALERE.
   Who's coming here?
BEJART.

                  Prince Conti.

VALERE.

                           Is that true??

(Bejart nods.)
   Good Lord! Am I presentable? MY TEETH!! –
(Opening his mouth.)
   Do they look crooked? Is there dirt beneath
(Holding out his hands.)
   My fingernails? My doublet – does it smell?

I've shown that I take criticism well,
So *please* be brutal, *heap* me with abuse!
Assume that I'm exceedingly obtuse ...
ELOMIRE.
(O, what a leap of the imagination!)
(Servants and Dorine rush in and begin to prepare the room for Prince Conti's entrance.)
BEJART.   *(To Elomire.)*
It's not the time to force a confrontation!
The Prince might hear us ...
ELOMIRE.

                              Which would be ideal!
Well, after all, he did arrange this meal
Intending (so you led me to believe
Before you plucked that writ out of your sleeve)
To introduce us to a candidate
Whom we'd be trusted to evaluate;
Not someone whom, despite what we might say,
Would be imposed upon us anyway!
The very thought that we're not *worth* consulting
Should strike you as sufficiently insulting
To tell the Prince, as I will, face to face,
Exactly how we feel about this case.
(Bejart, on the verge of protesting, is interrupted by a booming organ chord signalling the entrance of Prince Conti; Valere, seeing the Prince's shadow before anyone else, exclaims — or rather howls — the piercing hosanna "MY LIEGE!!" as the curtain falls.)

55

ACT TWO

The action continues. As the curtain rises, Valere is dropping to his knees before the Prince.

VALERE.   *(Shrieking.)*
    MY LIEGE!! MY SOVEREIGN!! IS IT TRULY THOU??
ELOMIRE.   *(Bows head.)*
    Good day, Your Grace.
BEJART.   *(Bows head.)*
                My lord.
VALERE.   *(Virtually prostrating himself in the salaam position.)*
                Then let me bow
So *deeply* that, by bowing anymore,
I'd be completely prostrate on the floor.
PRINCE.
    Good day to you ...
VALERE.
              For could I but descend
A fraction lower than you see me bend,
A fraction lower I would bend indeed!
PRINCE.
    My thanks.
VALERE.
          So *low* ...
PRINCE.
              But really: there's no need!
VALERE.
    ... that "low" would seem ... comparatively high!
ELOMIRE.   *(To Valere.)*
    Get up, for heaven's sake.
VALERE.
             And yet I shy
When basking in thy autocratic glow
From using such a lowly word as "low."
BEJART.   *(Echoing Elomire.)*
    Stand up, Valere.

56

VALERE.
                    STAND UP!? THAT'S SACRILEGE!!
Already it's too great a privilege
To be facedown in close proximity
To one of such divine divinity!
PRINCE.
I'm overwhelmed. I'm truly overcome ...
VALERE.   *(Indicating the numbing effect that the salaam position
has on his legs and genuflecting wildly.)*
Admittedly my legs are getting numb,
But in my other bones, down to the marrow,
I feel thy presence *deeply*, noble pharaoh!
"In mine is thine, for thine and mine entwine" ...
(Eyes pop.)
My God! That was a *lapidary* line!
I'm speaking poetry out of the
(With a wink to Dorine.)
                                        blue:
A poetry, my King, inspired by you!
PRINCE.
I'm hardly King ...
VALERE.   *(Feigning incredulity.)*
                    Art thou not King of France!?
Thou *shouldst* be King!! Thou *shouldst* be King of France!!
PRINCE.
I'm grateful for your paeans, but I fear
That I have interrupted something here ...
VALERE.
Impossible, my sultan!
ELOMIRE.
                    Not at all.
In fact – why were you waiting in the hall?
You should have come in straightaway, my lord.
PRINCE.
O, no. I think that would have been untoward.
Besides, I've been here longer than you know!
When I arrived a half an hour ago
Your troupe, assembled in the dining room,

Described how suddenly (and I assume
How anxiously) Bejart, Valere and you
Dashed off to have a private interview.
I urged them thus, as far as I was able,
To please remain discreetly at the table,
So you'd be free to form a pure reaction
Unvexed by any ripples of distraction.
And yet I broke the rule myself, you see?
Bedeviled by my curiosity
I simply couldn't keep from interfering:
I'm much too eager at the thought of hearing
Exactly how your *tête-à-tête* concluded.
And I don't mean to leave Bejart excluded!
He's part of this as well, let's not forget;
So shall I say your *"tête-à-tête-à-tête."*

VALERE.
    A *"TÊTE-À-TÊTE-A-TÊTE"*!! MY LORD, YOU'RE
      BRILLIANT!!
    There's not a wit more nimble or resilient
    Than that which you possess! Not now or ever!
    A *"tête-à-tête-à-tête"*:
(*Laughing and applauding.*)
                  O, *very* clever!
    Bra*vo*, my Sovereign! Daunting is the ease
    With which you weave linguistic tapestries!
    Astounding is your skill at verbal play:
    Each sentence seems an intricate ballet
    Where pronouns leap, and gerunds pirouette!
    That phrase, again...?

PRINCE.
               A *tête-à-tête-à-tête* ...

VALERE.
    A *TÊTE-À-TÊTE-A-TÊTE*! IT'S *TOO* DELICIOUS!
    My Lord, thou art so ...
(*Searching his mind for the perfect word.*)
              ... what? ... so ...
(*Positively blurting it out.*)
               ... LOVALITIOUS!! ...

A word I've just created on the fly!
For "LOVALITIOUS" seems to typify
(As common metaphors would fail to do)
The deep-down ... *LOVALITIOUSNESS* of you.
Yet were I bound by ordinary speech,
Thy every phrase I'd liken to a peach
Which thou hast coaxed (no mortal can say how)
To ripeness on the philologic bough;
Yes, like a shepherd to linguistic herds,
Thou hast – in short, my liege – a way with words.
PRINCE.
You honor me too much with this reply!
VALERE.
IMPOSSIBLE, O MONARCH OF THE SKY!
PRINCE.
But eloquence is *your* domain, not mine!
VALERE.
I've never heard more wisdom in *one* line!
Was everybody listening to that?
I take off my imaginary hat
To thee, my lord; I click my heels as well –
For how else could this tongue-tied actor tell
A wizard of the *logos (comme vous-même.)*
How totally he cherishes each gem
Thou effortlessly cast upon our ears ...
PRINCE.
That talent, though, is yours and Elomire's:
Because of it I wanted you to meet!
Alone, your plays, though great, seemed incomplete,
And, therefore, I was driven to know whether
I could, by bringing both of you together,
Create a whole out of your separate arts
Which might surpass the sum of all its parts.
VALERE.
Breathe not my name with that of Elomire:
I'm bound to earth, he skirts the stratosphere
(As playwright *and* as actor, brilliant, clearly –
Where I am but a brilliant actor, merely)

My couplets tend to lack the common touch,
A vulgar knack I envy overmuch
In masters like our darling Elomire ...
ELOMIRE.
Don't call me "darling"! Ever!
VALERE.

                    Sorry, dear ...
Well! *That* was rather on the snippy side!
I seemed to have misjudged your sense of pride!
Still quaking at my quibbles even yet?
Don't crucify yourself on vinaigrette –
I didn't mean to stir up such ado!
To punish me for being frank with you
Seems – I don't know – a wee bit juvenile.
"A MAN SHOULD TAKE HIS LICKINGS WITH A SMILE."
PRINCE.
I know that line ...
VALERE.

              But can you pin it down?
PRINCE.   *(Gasping.)*
Of course...!
VALERE.

      That's right.
PRINCE.

          Your play...!
VALERE.

                The Dying Clown!
PRINCE.
THE DYING CLOWN! I *LOVED* THAT!
VALERE.

              Most agree.
That you remember it surprises me.
PRINCE.
Remember it? I wept throughout Act Two!
It's where you showed that clowns have feelings, too –
How mirth with sorrow in each soul competes ...
VALERE.
I leave such chitchat to the exegetes.

I'm useless as a critic – I *create!*
An artist's at a loss to explicate
His raw ideas; to him, they're heaven-sent.
"That clowns have feelings" ... *is* that what I meant?
Perhaps. And if I did ...
(Small giggle at the realization.)
                              ... it's rather *good.*
(Guffaw of self-delight.)
PRINCE.   *(To Elomire.)*
      Have you not seen it?
ELOMIRE.

                              No.

PRINCE.

                    O, then you *should.*
BEJART.
      I saw it.
VALERE.   *(Grovelingly acknowledging the remark as if Bejart had
just said "it was a work of genius.")*
                    Thank you. *Thank* you.
PRINCE.

                              Really, where?
BEJART.
      A year ago in Brussels at a fair.
VALERE.
      O *NO!!* NOT *BRUSSELS!!* I WAS OFF THAT NIGHT!!
      I had a chest cold and – to be polite –
      Let's call it "something wrong beneath my waist"!
      You saw me *then?* O God! I feel disgraced!
PRINCE.
      Well, why don't you make up for it right now?
VALERE.
      Make up for it, my Sovereign? Tell me how!
PRINCE.
      By doing just a tidbit from the play.
VALERE.
      O no no no, my lord! O, nay nay nay!
PRINCE.
      But *please* ...

VALERE.

O nein! O nicht! O niente!

PRINCE.

Why?

VALERE.

I can't Your Grace.

PRINCE.

Why not?

VALERE.

Because I'm shy.
And out of context it would be ...

PRINCE.

O boo!
I'm asking for a simple line or two!

VALERE.

Without the cow ... they wouldn't understand ...

PRINCE.

This isn't a request, it's a command.

VALERE.

Command, you say? Well, since I'm at your beck,
I'll smooth the hackles rising on my neck
And grant, unwillingly, a brief recital
Of Baba's tearful farewell to his title
As *"clune extraordinaire"* du *"Cirque Soleil"*:
This is the final couplet of the play.
(Sniffs and extends handkerchief.)
"CAST DOWN MY POLKA-DOTTED PANTALOONS,
MY RUBBER LIPS, MY COLORFUL BALLOONS" ...
And then I blow my nose and kiss the pigeon ...
(Kisses cupped hands and releases imaginary pigeon.)
Well, anyway, that's just a tiny smidgen
From something that took decades to perfect.
(The Prince looks to Elomire and Bejart, who are clearly unimpressed.)

PRINCE.   *(Slightly embarrassed.)*

You'll understand I mean no disrespect
By telling you, Valere, that, while delightful,
The Dying Clown seems somewhat less insightful

(And Baba's death less poignantly sublime)
When one observes the scene a second time.
VALERE.   *(Swept by a wave of panic, he blurts out.)*
But that was my *INTENTION!!*
PRINCE.   *(Genuinely.)*
                                          Was it!?
VALERE.   *(Clearly relieved and encouraged.)*
                                    YESSSSSSS!!
How gratifying, Lord, that you should guess!
Departing from theatrical tradition,
The play is so designed that each rendition
Deliberately lessens our esteem
Until, oppressed by every blotch and seam,
We're stunned by the respect that first we had
For something which is so supremely bad.
PRINCE.
You mean the play's *intended* to go *stale!?*
VALERE.
To be successful, Lord, the play must fail.
PRINCE.
But that's *ingenious!*
VALERE.
                    Sire, I do my best.
(And he staggers away, slightly wounded.)
PRINCE.
Why, Elomire: you must be so impressed!
Imagine planting in a play's construction
The seeds which guarantee its self-destruction!
The concept seems both daring and nouveau!
Could you have thought of it? Be honest.
ELOMIRE.   *(He's onto something; his mind is racing ahead.)*
                                          No.
PRINCE.
Voilà! This news exceeds my expectations!
I'm dazzled by dramatic innovations!
ELOMIRE.
Still won't you show, Valere, how you excel
At forms much more conventional as well?

PRINCE. *(To Elomire, excited.)*
Another play?
ELOMIRE. *(Matter-of-fact.)*
I'd *love* to see him in it.
PRINCE. *(To Valere, "I told you so.")*
Did you hear *that*?
BEJART. *(To Elomire, perplexed.)*
Excuse me ...
VALERE. *(Suspicious.)*
Wait a minute ...
ELOMIRE. *(To Bejart, sotto voce.)*
Have faith, my friend.
PRINCE. *(Enjoying his prescience about the Elomire-Valere team.)*
I *knew* that this would work!
ELOMIRE. *(To Valere.)*
GO ON!
VALERE. *(Nervous.)*
No no.
PRINCE. *(To Valere.)*
YOU MUST!
BEJART. *(To Elomire, sotto voce.)*
Are you berserk...?
ELOMIRE. *(To Bejart, sotto voce and final.)*
Just trust me.
PRINCE. *(To Valere.)*
Now!
VALERE. *(Trapped.)*
Well ... could'st thou be specific?
PRINCE.
O, do that thing you do that's so terrific ...
The ... what's-it-called ... come on ... you know the play!
VALERE.
Might Lordship fling a *tiny* clue my way?
PRINCE.
The one that stands out like a shining star...!
VALERE.
That *could* mean my entire repertoire!

PRINCE.
    No, no. I mean your masterpiece, Valere.
VALERE.
    Which *one?*
PRINCE.
                You did it in the public square
    Six weeks ago ...
VALERE.
                You don't mean *Death by Cheese!*
PRINCE.
    No, that's not it.
VALERE.
                The Life of Damocles?
PRINCE.
    Another one ...
VALERE.   *(Snapping his fingers, thinking he's got it.)*
                The Bishop's Macaroon!!
PRINCE.
    Another ...
VALERE.
                Well, there's *Goddess from the Moon* ...
(Prince squints as if that may be it. Valere supplies more detail.)
    Where I get all dressed up as Aphrodite...?
PRINCE.   *(Waves it off.)*
    No, it's the one where you *don't* wear a nightie.
VALERE.   *(Realizing.)*
    O, *now* I think I know which one it is ...
(Sniffs and extends handkerchief.)
    The Parable of Two Boys from Cadiz!
PRINCE.
    *MY GOD! THAT'S IT! YOU'RE RIGHT! THAT'S WHAT
        IT IS!!*
    THE PARABLE OF TWO BOYS FROM CADIZ!!
VALERE.
    But Lord, I can't ...
ELOMIRE.
                Why not?

VALERE.

O, please don't ask.
To do it *well* is such a grueling task:
It takes the most amazing concentration!
ELOMIRE.
Then we'll allow for lack of preparation.
VALERE.
I'd need my juggling balls and my prosthesis ...
PRINCE.
Why can't you just suggest them through mimesis?
VALERE.   *(With his eyes on Elomire.)*
You've missed the point, my lord, if I may dare.
My props are in my gunnysack out there –
It's not for want of them that I resist;
It's more that I'm a staunch perfectionist
Who, bristling at the slightest compromise,
Won't utter *"faute de mieux"* until he dies!
How quaint that sounds in this corrupted age
When half-baked twaddle dominates our stage,
But lower standards make me feel *degraded.*
I thus refuse (and cannot be persuaded)
To vulgarize a work which at the core
Demands a day of preparation – MORE! –
A week, perhaps, if I'm to get it right.
Hence I cannot fulfill your wish tonight!
PRINCE.
Then I'm afraid you're finished here, Valere.
VALERE.
I'll need about three minutes to prepare.
(He bows kissing his fingertips, making a backwards exit.)
PRINCE.
Ah! Wonderful! I'm glad you've changed your mind!
Bejart and Elomire, I think you'll find
The Parable of Two Boys from Cadiz
Is everything that I have said it is!
ELOMIRE.
I long for it to start ...

PRINCE.

In fact, Bejart,
Go fetch the others – you know where they are –
I want the troupe to see this!

BEJART.

Very well.

(Pointedly, to Elomire.)
I'm sure if Elomire decides to tell
Your Lordship of the words we shared alone,
He'll honor my opinion as his own.

(Glancing at Elomire, he bows and exits. Dorine exits.)

PRINCE.
I'm sure he will.

(To Elomire.)

Now what was *that* about?

ELOMIRE.
O, never mind, my lord. I highly doubt
Such trivia would interest you at all.

PRINCE.   *(Excitedly.)*
Then what about Valere? Did he enthrall
The company at dinner? Was he witty?
Did he recite that syncopated ditty
About the gnome whose trousers scrape the floor...?

ELOMIRE.   *(Nodding, pained.)*
He did indeed, my lord, and *so* much more.

(As if to say "what planet does he come from?")
Where did you *find* him?

PRINCE.

In the public square!

Can you *imagine*? In the open air –
A talent of *that* magnitude...!

ELOMIRE.

It's frightening.

PRINCE.
When I first saw him I was struck by lightning!
A voice inside of me cried out "NOW HERE,
NOW HERE'S A MAN WHO *MUST* MEET ELOMIRE!

A COMMON STREET CLOWN, TRUE, BUT WHAT
    A GIFT!
AND CERTAINLY THE TROUPE COULD USE A LIFT!"
ELOMIRE.
    A lift? What sort of lift?
PRINCE.

    A ... "perking-up."

(Pause.)
    For several weeks now I've been working up
    The courage to reprove you, Elomire,
    For faults caused (unavoidably, I fear)
    By too much time unchallenged – by *stagnation!*
    The troupe seems listless in my estimation:
    Not daring as it was a year ago!
    Remember how you strove, with every show,
    To break *some* rule, to shatter *some* convention?
    What happened to the talent for invention
    That earned you your exalted reputation
    In all the provinces throughout the nation
    As rival to the genius of Corneille?
ELOMIRE.
    If you're as disappointed as you say
    What's needed to improve the situation?
PRINCE.
    New blood to stimulate the circulation!
    A year at court has undermined your morals:
    You've grown content to rest upon your laurels
    As if afflicted by some dread ennui.
    Valere will challenge your complacency!
    Between two men of talent, competition
    Can be a most desirable condition
    For it propels them both to greater heights
    Until, producing myriad delights
    Which, separately, they *never* would have done,
    The rivals come to see themselves as "one" –
    A team, depending each upon the other!
    Tonight you've met your spiritual brother:

A man whose gifts provide (it seems to me)
A rare and welcome opportunity.
ELOMIRE.
Perhaps less opportune, my lord, than rare:
I'd welcome anyone *except* Valere!
If that's too blunt, forgive me, but it's true:
I see no purpose in deceiving you ...
PRINCE.   *(Completely incredulous.)*
Deceiving me? You mean you didn't *like* him?
ELOMIRE.
I mean that not to *strangle* him or *strike* him
Required unbelievable restraint ...
PRINCE.
Good God!
ELOMIRE.
                    WAIT! That's the least of my complaint!
PRINCE.
The LEAST?
ELOMIRE.
                    The *LEAST!*
PRINCE.
                                        Now don't be cross ...
ELOMIRE.
                                                            But Lord ...
PRINCE.
I'm not insisting that he be adored,
But only that ...
ELOMIRE.
                    WE'RE ... NOT... COMMUNICATING ...
PRINCE.
... You overlook what you find "irritating"
About Valere ...
ELOMIRE.   *(Tensely, pained.)*
                    But NOTHING would remain!
PRINCE.
You're being churlish!
ELOMIRE.
                    Lord, would I complain ...

69

PRINCE.   *(Cutting Elomire off, haughtily.)*
    Valere, you either could or could not see,
    Is really something of an oddity ...
ELOMIRE.
    I could see that ...
PRINCE.

                            He is, and there are few,
    An *"idiot savant"!*
ELOMIRE.
                            That's *partly* true.
PRINCE.
    That's *partly* true?
ELOMIRE.
                            I mean I *half* agree!
PRINCE.
    Explain yourself!
ELOMIRE.
                            How pointed can one be?
    I think the man's an idiot
PRINCE.   *(Completing this phrase as if they were in agreement.)*
                            — savant.

ELOMIRE.
    No no, my lord. A chucklehead
PRINCE.

                                            — savant.

ELOMIRE.
    No no, my lord. Not *"chucklehead savant."*
    Just chucklehead. Just idiot
PRINCE.
                            — savant.

ELOMIRE.
    The man's a cretin, Lord!
PRINCE.
                            O no no no!

ELOMIRE.
    A nincompoop! A boob!
PRINCE.
                        That isn't so!

You've totally misread him, Elomire...!
ELOMIRE.
　　I haven't!
PRINCE.
　　　　　　Quite egregiously, I fear.
　　In fact, I'm nothing short of stupefied
　　That you, an artist, trained to look *inside*,
　　Should base your views on *superficial* flaws.
　　It's one of life's profound, unwritten laws
　　That people whom you least expect it of
　　May harbor, like a hand inside a glove,
　　Some mystery, some talent left unproved
　　Because the glove has never been removed!
　　The baker's wife, for instance: just suppose
　　A prima ballerina's in her toes!
　　The butcher: might he not, behind his hams,
　　Be peerless at unscrambling anagrams?
　　Perhaps the milkman loves Etruscan art;
　　The barber may know Ptolemy by heart;
　　The priest might be a stunning acrobat;
　　Well, one could just go on and on like that ...
　　The lesson here is that the naked eye
　　Is often insufficient to espy
　　The wealth of *natural* talent left unseen
　　Unless one probes beneath or checks between.
　　You haven't really looked at this Valere ...
ELOMIRE.
　　I have, my lord ...
PRINCE.
　　　　　　　Not deep enough to bare
　　The soul of his achievement, which transcends
　　Theatrical performance and extends
　　To realms the likes of which you'd never guess:
　　He taught the King of Sweden to play chess!
ELOMIRE.
　　Who told you that?
PRINCE.
　　　　　　He told me!

71

ELOMIRE.

O, my *God!*

And you *believed* him?
PRINCE.

Yes – is that so odd?
(Irritated and impatient with this argument, he cuts it off.)
I'd HOPED that you'd have liked him as a man.
Still, you can *work* together ...
ELOMIRE.

NO!

PRINCE.

YES ...

PRINCE.   *(Deadly.)*

you can.
By which I mean you will. Or, otherwise –
(Mounting frustration.)
If you can't make *one tiny compromise*
Respecting ME –
(A flash of anger.)

then get your troupe and go!
(Petulance.)
You have no *right* to flout my wishes so!
I CANNOT STAND THIS IN YOU ELOMIRE!
I've always given you your freedom here
Supporting you like kings when half the time
Your work's too dark or dense or fails to rhyme
Or makes no sense, or takes strange points of view.
This man has gifts that will inspire you!
Now that's what *I* believe – and, in the end
MY say-so is what matters. Why, my friend,
Are you so stubborn?! You've not seen his play.
(Hapless, uncomprehending.)
Why is it so IMPORTANT, anyway?
He's just ONE MAN ...
(Princely.)

whose talent pleases me.
(Stern and final.)
Now you'll accept him as a courtesy ...

No less than that which I have shown to you
By setting up this meal ...
ELOMIRE.

                    If that were true
My judgment would be honored, not ignored.
BUT *THIS* –
(He produces the writ.)

        IS *THIS* A COURTESY, MY LORD?!
I never thought you'd show me such contempt!
I'd fooled myself to think we were exempt
From pressures of this sort since (from the start)
You've honored me, my thoughts, my troupe, my art
In such a rare, uncompromising way,
That naturally we've struggled to repay
Your kindness with new work that's just as rare.
But now you force upon us this ... VALERE ...
And tell me I should get my troupe and *go?!*
Have we so *failed* you?
PRINCE.   *(Moved by this.)*

                No. Of course not. No.
It pains me that you say that when it's clear
How deeply I admire you, Elomire.
This troupe has been, for me, a source of pride ...
ELOMIRE.
Then why not, please, let *all* of us decide?!
And why not let this *Parable* of his,
This ...
PRINCE.

      Parable of Two Boys from Cadiz
ELOMIRE.
Be crucial in determining his fate.
PRINCE.
I've *seen* it, though. It's charming.
ELOMIRE.

               Yes, but wait:
Remember when you watched *The Dying Clown*
A *second* time you felt ...

PRINCE.

That's true ...

ELOMIRE.

... let down.

PRINCE.
But he explained that brilliantly.

ELOMIRE.

What's more,
He acts *alone,* my lord, not in a corps
Of players like our own, where all take part.
His monologue's a selfish pseudo-art
Which puts the man himself above the group.

PRINCE.
I take your point.

ELOMIRE. *(The idea really clicking in.)*
Why not ... allow the troupe
To join him in this *Parable* and see
If he could truly *serve* the company
Instead of ...
(Expansive.)
taking over!

PRINCE.

I don't know ...

ELOMIRE.
A joint performance cannot fail to show
How much an asset or a threat he'd be.

PRINCE.
A *threat?!* But that's absurd hyperbole!

ELOMIRE.   *(In sincere pain.)*
He'd RUIN us.

PRINCE.   *(Intrigued.)*
You *mean* it, Elomire.

ELOMIRE.
I couldn't be more serious ...

PRINCE.

O, dear!
(He walks U. and thinks about it. Then, with gentle, eerie sarcasm, bemused by the fraught situation and his power to affect it.)

You'd think the world itself were at an end!
(Chortles, rather menacingly.)
You're funny you're so serious, my friend.
(Half-smiling.)
Commitment to your art deserves respect,
(Fast and beseechingly.)
But not when it compels you to reject
As *"monstrous"* any change that fails to suit
Your own designs –
(Incredulous.)
                       and *this* seems so minute;
(Sighing, frustrated but with respect.)
Still, rigidly you press your point of view.
(Brief pause. He studies Elomire. Then – shaking his head – ambiguously, so that his words are simultaneously affectionate and chilling.)
Whatever am I going to do with you?
(The Prince laughs, surprisingly, inappropriately. Then, dead serious, he gestures for Elomire to come close. A smile creeps back around the corners of his lips and he snatches the writ from Elomire's hands, tearing it up and throwing the pieces into the air like confetti.)
All right then. Very well.

ELOMIRE.   *(Sighs, tremendously relieved.)*
                      Our thanks, my lord!

PRINCE.
But let us have a *mutual* accord:
If I review him in this different light
You must be less *insistent* that you're right.
My mind is open – tell me yours is, too.

ELOMIRE.   *(Under the strain of a bargain.)*
I like to think, my lord, that's always true.

PRINCE.   *(Satisfied enough.)*
Then this should be great fun, don't you agree?
We'll neither praise nor fault too eagerly ...

(Enter Bejart and his sister Madeleine, followed by De Brie and his wife Catherine, and Du Parc and his wife Marquise-Therese. They are talking amongst themselves, but Bejart overhears the Prince's last sentence.)

BEJART.

Um ... finding fault with whom?

PRINCE.

Ah! Here they are!

BEJART.

With whom? With us?

PRINCE.

O heavens no, Bejart!

(*Generally.*)

COME IN! COME IN! WE HAVE A TREAT IN STORE!
BUT FIRST I NEED YOUR HELP TO CLEAR THE
FLOOR –
A SPACE RIGHT OVER THERE, I THINK, WILL DO ...

BEJART.

Is it all right ...

MADELEINE.

Excuse me, Lord ...

DU PARC.

May I request ...

MARQUISE-THERESE.

A moment, please ...

DE BRIE.

I wish to speak ...

CATHERINE.

Would you allow ...

PRINCE.

I CAN'T HEAR *ALL* OF YOU!!

BEJART.

I understand my lord ...

MADELEINE.

Then let me quickly say ...

DU PARC.

He's absolutely right ...

MARQUISE-THERESE.

It's vital that you know.

DE BRIE.

Be quiet everyone ...

CATHERINE.

I simply want to ask ...

PRINCE.

PLEASE! SETTLE DOWN!

BEJART.

You heard him! Settle down ...

MADELEINE.

Be quiet everyone ...

DU PARC.

Of course: but if I may ...

MARQUISE-THERESE.

I would if there were time ...

DE BRIE.

The point I want to make ...

CATHERINE.

He can't hear anything ...

PRINCE.

YOU'RE MAKING SUCH A DIN! YOUR VOICES
DROWN

BEJART.

He can't hear anything!

MADELEINE.

Just let me talk, all right?

DU PARC.

Good gracious! Hold your tongues!

MARQUISE-THERESE.

Would everyone shut up!?

DE BRIE.

You're stepping on my speech!

CATHERINE.

An utter waste of time!

PRINCE.

EACH OTHER OUT COMPLETELY! WHAT A
CLAMOR!

MADELEINE.

BUT LORD!

DU PARC.

BUT LORD!

MARQUISE-THERESE.

BUT LORD!

PRINCE.

                                 IT'S LIKE A HAMMER
    POUNDING ON MY SKULL!!
DE BRIE:

                       BUT LORD!!

PRINCE.

                              BE *STILL!!*

(Pause, to gather control.)
    Now: one by one.
BEJART.

                My lord, despite the skill

MADELEINE.

                My lord, we've had our fill

DU PARC.

                My lord, Therese is ill

MARQUISE-THERESE.

                My lord, I have a chill

DE BRIE.

                My lord, while quite a thrill

CATHERINE:

                My lord, though it's your will

BEJART.
    Valere has shown.
MADELEINE.
    Of him tonight ...
DU PARC.
    I'm sad to say ...
MARQUISE-THERESE.
    And need to rest ...
DE BRIE.
    To see Valere ...
CATHERINE.
    That we remain ...
PRINCE.
    THIS REALLY IS IMPOSSIBLE!
PRINCE.

                       BE *QUIET!!*
YOU'RE BABBLING LIKE A RABBLE IN A RIOT ...

BEJART.
   Well, if we are ...
MADELEINE:
   Whose fault is *that?*
DU PARC.
   But that's because ...
MARQUISE-THERESE.
   You're blaming me?
DE BRIE.
   I know, I know ...
CATHERINE.
   But, please, my lord ...
PRINCE.

   I'M TELLING YOU TO STOP!!

(Pause.)
   NOW: why don't we just take this from the top.
   Who wants to speak?
BEJART.
               I DO!
MADELEINE.
               I DO!
DU PARC.
                  I DO!
MARQUISE-THERESE.
                  I DO!
DE BRIE.
                     I DO!
CATHERINE.
                     I DO!
BEJART.
   With your permission ...
MADELEINE.
   If Lordship pleases ...
DU PARC.
   As I was saying ...
MARQUISE-THERESE.
   I think it's vital ...

DE BRIE.
    My instinct tells me ...
CATHERINE.
    It isn't proper ...
PRINCE.

> *SILENCE! ALL OF YOU!*

Bejart. Can you account for this display?

(Bejart and Madeleine peel off D. to the Prince; the other members of the troupe cross up to Elomire and confront him.)

BEJART.
    My lord, the troupe is in a rush to say
MADELEINE.   *(Jumping in, theatrically enthusiastic.)*
    We're grateful
DU PARC.   *(Confronting Elomire.)*

> WE DEMAND AN EXPLANATION.

ELOMIRE.   *(Insouciant.)*
    FOR WHAT?
PRINCE.   *(Genuinely, to the Bejarts.)*

> For what?

DE BRIE.   *(To Elomire.)*

> THIS AWKWARD SITUATION!

BEJART.   *(To the Prince.)*
    For having had the chance to meet
MADELEINE.   *(Jumping in again; expressed with a certain horror.)*

> that man.

MARQUISE-THERESE.   *(As Elomire continues to feign ignorance.)*
    DON'T SHRUG AS IF WE'RE CRAZY!
BEJART.   *(Indicating Madeleine.)*

> She's a fan ...

MADELEINE.   *(Too eager.)*
    Who wouldn't be.
ELOMIRE.   *(Querulously, to the troupe.)*
    YOU ALL SEEM SO EXCITED.
BEJART.   *(To the Prince.)*
    It's late, though ...

DU PARC.   *(To Elomire.)*
                    WE WERE TOLD THAT YOU INVITED
THAT *FOOL* TO DO HIS ... WHAT?
BEJART.   *(Continuing, to the Prince.)*
                                        ... and, as it is,
ELOMIRE.
THE PARABLE OF TWO BOYS FROM CADIZ }
BEJART.
The Parable of Two Boys from Cadiz
BEJART.
Could never be unstintingly admired.
ELOMIRE.   *(To the troupe.)*
I DID SUGGEST IT, YES.
MADELEINE.   *(Nervously yawning.)*
                        We're all too tired ...
DE BRIE.   *(Extremely displeased, to Elomire.)*
WHAT *ARE* YOU UP TO?
ELOMIRE.
                    TRUST ME.
BEJART.   *(To the Prince.)*
                        Yawn yawn yawn!
CATHERINE.   *(To Elomire.)*
JUST TELL US, *PLEASE!*
(Elomire simply holds his hands up reassuringly.)
MADELEINE.   *(To the Prince.)*
                    Indeed, it's nearly dawn
MARQUISE-THERESE.   *(To Elomire.)*
WE *HAVE* TO WATCH THIS? *NOW?!*
(Elomire nods confidently.)
PRINCE.   *(To the Bejarts.)*
                        It's barely eight!
ELOMIRE.
NOT MERELY WATCH – YOU'LL ALL PARTICIPATE!
*(The members of the troupe are stunned, astonishment silencing their
confusion for a moment. The Prince, having heard Elomire make this
pronouncement, breaks away from the Bejarts and crosses up to
Elomire and the troupe.)*

PRINCE.
>Yes! Wonderful! Did everybody hear?!
>A grand suggestion, thanks to Elomire:
>It's *his* idea that you should all ... "join in."

(The heads of the astonished members of the troupe swivel back to Elomire.)

ELOMIRE.   *(Eagerly.)*
>There's no time like the present to begin
>To test how well our new-formed team will do.

(Indicating the Prince.)
>Whenever others voice a point of view
>That's different from my own, I ...

(He bows to the Prince.)

>   think again.
>Valere, I realize now, like many men
>Has flaws which might disguise great talent ... MIGHT!
>The Prince has seen it – could it be, *he's* right?!

(Silence. Slapping hands together.)
>Well,

(The Du Parcs turn U., plotting; the De Bries, dumbstruck, hover nervously between cheer and anguish – they are confused, caged animals.)

>   acting in this

(Deferential, to the Prince.)
>   "masterpiece" that is
>*The Parable of Two Boys from Cadiz*
>Will help us get a feel ...

DU PARC.   *(Turns and interjects.)*
>   UMMMMMM!

PRINCE.
>   Yes, Du Parc?

DU PARC.
>Therese is ill, my lord. Her tongue's gone dark.

PRINCE.
>Her tongue's gone dark?

DU PARC.
>   Yes, very.

PRINCE.

Let me see.

(*Marquise-Therese sticks out her tongue.*)

DU PARC.

It's darker than a normal tongue should be ...

PRINCE.

Well if it is, so what?

ELOMIRE.

Precisely!

BEJART.

PLEASE!

(*Bejart takes Madeleine's hand and they cross to Elomire. Du Parc continues to address the Prince. The three following conversations take place simultaneously. They are synchronized to be of exactly equal length and should be recited in an established rhythm, like a fugue.*)

DU PARC.
The point is that it
might be some
disease
That left untreated
could, for all I
know
Infect the lot of us...!

PRINCE.
She's healthy,
though!

DU PARC.
Perhaps! But since we're
not completely sure
Prevention is the most
effective cure!
She must be put to bed!
And, as it is,
The Parable of...?

PRINCE.
... Two Boys from Cadiz ...

MADELEINE.   (*Hissing
whisper.*)
Would you be quiet!
Can't you see that
she's
Attempting to convince
the Prince to spare
The troupe from this
recital by Valere?

ELOMIRE.
By feigning illness? What
can that achieve
Except, at best, a very
short reprieve?
Just tell the truth as I've
already done ...

BEJART.
I hope you didn't speak
for everyone!

83

DU PARC.
Would better be
performed on some
occasion
When we would feel
less threated by
contagion.

ELOMIRE.
Well if I did, would
there be some
objection?
MADELEINE.
There would if it
results in our
ejection!

DORINE.   (Entering, speaking as Du Parc says
"Perhaps!")
SHOE!
CATHERINE.
I'm sorry?
DE BRIE.
What
CATHERINE.
Did you say "SHOE"?
DE BRIE.
I didn't, no.
CATHERINE.
Well if it wasn't you
Then who just said it ...
DORINE.
SHOE! ...
DE BRIE.
Why it's Dorine!
CATHERINE.
Come in!
DE BRIE.   (To Dorine.)
Did you say "SHOE"?
CATHERINE.
What could it mean?
DE BRIE.
HELLO! HELLO! HELLO! ...
(His voice emerging from the babble.)
HELLO! HELLO!

84

DE BRIE.   *(Clapping hands together.)*
　　ATTENTION!! HUSH!! Does everybody know
　　Dorine is standing here and saying "SHOE"!?
CATHERINE.
　　Indeed she is...!
DU PARC.
　　She's saying "SHOE"...?
DE BRIE.
　　　　　　　　　　　BE QUIET, ALL OF YOU!
　　Come in, Dorine. Be careful with your dress.
(Dorine descends the step.)
　　You have a little message for us, yes?
(She nods.)
　　What is it, dear?
(She opens her mouth to speak but, teasingly, doesn't.)
　　　　　　　　　　　Just *say* it please Dorine!
DORINE.
　　SHOE!
DE BRIE.
　　　　　Shoe–WHAT!?
DU PARC.
　　　　　　　　　Shoe–*WHAT!?*
CATHERINE.
　　　　　　　　　　　　Well, "SHOE" could mean
　　Shoe–LACE.
DE BRIE.
　　　　　　Or–STRING!
CATHERINE.
　　　　　　　　　　Or–MAKER!
DE BRIE.
　　　　　　　　　　　　　Are we right?
(Dorine shakes her head no.)
CATHERINE.
　　Shoe–HORN?
DU PARC.
　　　　　Shoe–SIZE?
DE BRIE.
　　　　　　　Shoe–LENGTH?

DU PARC.

                                                       Shoe—WIDTH?
CATHERINE.

                                                                   Shoe—
                       HEIGHT?
(Dorine continues to shake her head no.)
DU PARC.
    Or is it "SHOO-SHOO-SHOO, BEGONE! GET OUT!"?
(Dorine shakes her head no.)
PRINCE.   *(To Madeleine.)*
    Now what the devil is *this* all about?
MADELEINE.
    Dorine, my lord, is going through a phase.
PRINCE.
    O, not *again*...!
DE BRIE.
                       Is there another phrase
    That might make sense of "SHOE"?
MADELEINE.
                                    And it's unique:
CATHERINE.
    Shoe—SOLE?
DU PARC.
                   Shoe—POLISH?
DORINE.
                                   SHOE!
MADELEINE.
                                   She will not speak
    Except in monosyllables that rhyme!
DE BRIE.
    Shoe—TOE?
PRINCE.
               At least that's better than the time
    She hummed E *flat* incessantly, remember?
DU PARC.
    Shoe—HEEL?
MADELEINE.   *(Nodding.)*
               Or worse, that fortnight in December

                              86

(Dorine shakes her head "no" impatiently in response to Du Parc, and then begins to mime exaggerated emotions and perform wild gesticulations.)

When all she did from dawn to dusk was whirl!
PRINCE.

Just ... spun around?
(Madeleine nods.)
CATHERINE.

Shoe–LACE?

(Dorine shakes her head no impatiently and becomes even more exaggerated.)
PRINCE.

Peculiar girl!

DE BRIE.

No, "LACE" was said already ...
PRINCE.

What's she *doing?*

CATHERINE.

Perhaps the word is "ISSUE" or "ESCHEWING" ...
(Dorine shakes her head no and continues to gesture wildly.)
MADELEINE.

She's acting out a clue ...
DU PARC.

I'VE SEEN ENOUGH!

DU PARC.

TO PUT UP WITH THIS ADOLESCENT STUFF
DORINE.   *(She sings the word.)*

Shooooooooooooooooooooooooooe!!!
DU PARC.

... IS MORE THAN I CAN BEAR!
(Fanning Marquise-Therese in a chair.)

... Therese is *dying!*

(Marquise-Therese coughs theatrically.)
DE BRIE.

Dorine is SINGING!
(Dorine, nodding vigorously, gives a rolling hand gesture, as in cha-

87

rades, to encourage similar suggestions; immediately she goes up on point, and starts to ballet dance while continuing to assume grand expressions.)

PRINCE. *(To Du Parc.)*

                Everybody's trying ...

DU PARC.

   WILL SOMEONE CALL A DOCTOR!?

PRINCE. *(To Du Parc.)*

                     ... so should *you!*

DE BRIE.

   She's singing and she's ... LOOK! ... she's *dancing,* too!

DORINE. *(In a histrionic voice.)*

                         SHOE!!

CATHERINE.

   And chewing up the scenery!

PRINCE. *(Guessing.)*

              A *PLAY!?*

DE BRIE.

   A *FARCE?*

CATHERINE.

       An *OPERETTA?*

PRINCE.

             A *BALLET?*

MADELEINE.

   She shouldn't be indulged ...

DE BRIE.

                They *ALL* apply?

DU PARC.

   IS THERE A DOCTOR IN THE HOUSE ...!?

(Dorine's vigorous nodding to Catherine's question causes everyone to look at one another.)

PRINCE.

                    O MY!

CATHERINE.

                    O MY!

DE BRIE.

                    O MY!

DE BRIE.
   Well if it's *all* those things, what could it be?
CATHERINE.
   A *FESTIVAL*, a...?
DORINE.

                        SHOE!!

MADELEINE.

                        Don't look at me...!

PRINCE.
   A *GALA?*
DU PARC.
                  Lord! I beg you ...
CATHERINE.

                        I don't know!

MARQUISE-THERESE.   *(Snapping out of her pretended stupor.)*
   FOR GOD'S SAKE, CAN'T YOU SEE THE WORD IS
      "SHOW"!?

*(Dorine leaps and gives her "on the nose" signal. The door swings
open. The troupe turns, gasps, screams. Blackout. Lights up quickly.
The members of the troupe are staring in disbelief at Valere, who is
costumed in a bizarre, wildly garish Harlequin outfit with an immense
fright wig. He crashes a pair of cymbals.)*

VALERE.
   IT'S SHOWTIME, *YES!* A MARVELOUS DEDUCTION!
(To Dorine.)
   I thank you for that splendid introduction
   (Although you might have simply said *"VOILÀ"*;
   Still, your way had a special *"je ne sais quoi ..."!)*
   But far *more* special is the gift I bear:
   Breathe in, my friends, there's magic in the air!
   Can you not smell that vague exotic scent
   Like mystic perfume from the Orient?
   'Tis but an intimation of the spell
   Cast forth by this enchanting tale I tell!
   MOVE BACK, YOU LOUTS! IT'S STUFFY AS A TOMB!
   MAKE WAY! GET OFF THE PLATFORM! GIVE ME
      ROOM!
   Go find a free *"francesca"* and stay seated

Until my presentation is completed.
No talking and no spitting, by the way:
There's nothing more disruptive to a play
Than hearing someone gab or ...
(Makes the ripe sound of coughing up phlegm.)
                                        ... bring up phlegm
When you're reciting your most precious gem!
(Suddenly aware that they are all staring at him, their jaws hanging open.)
Good Lord! What's everybody staring at?
DU PARC.
Your ...
VALERE.
            Yes? ...
DE BRIE.
                  Your ...
VALERE.
                        WHAT?
MADELEINE.
                              Your *COSTUME!*
VALERE.
                                          O yes, *that!*

Distinctive, no? It won two *huge* awards:
"The Golden Bobbin," and "The Silver Swords."
(It took twelve peasant girls six months to make!)
No, I'm just teasing you, for heaven's sake –
I patched it up myself from odds and ends!
But this is rather off the point, my friends ...
I've got some sheets. Take one and pass them round.
PRINCE.
What is it?
VALERE.
            It's the text. You see, I've found
That often the most beautiful invention
Is lost, or met with dull incomprehension
Unless the crowd can savor every word.
This lets them *read* along ...

PRINCE.

But you've not heard!

VALERE.

Heard what?

PRINCE.

They're going to *join* you!

VALERE.   *(Tensely.)*

In what way?

ELOMIRE.   *(Mischievously.)*

The troupe is going to join you in your play.

VALERE.   *(Slow turn, suspicious.)*

To ... *join* me?

ELOMIRE.

Yes.

VALERE.

You can't.

ELOMIRE.

Why not?

VALERE.   *(He begins re-collecting the scripts.)*

NO! NO!

My Lord, this is a strictly *one-man show*
Where I play every part, speak every line ...

PRINCE.

It's Elomire's idea, it isn't mine.

ELOMIRE.

It should be quite revealing in that light.

VALERE.   *(Genuinely distressed.)*

Another time perhaps, but not tonight;
I'm feeling too much pressure as it is ...

(Elomire clears his throat and reads from his script; Valere is losing control.)

ELOMIRE.

The Parable of Two Boys from Cadiz.

VALERE.   *(Pulling the script violently from Elomire's hands.)*

JUST GIVE ME THOSE!

(But Elomire is redistributing the other copies.)

PRINCE.   *(Getting comfortable.)*

No arguments! Let's go!

I'm sitting here and waiting for the show.
MADELEINE.
Will there be costumes for the troupe to wear?
VALERE.
With those hips? Hardly ...
PRINCE.

Start the play, Valere!
VALERE.
With *them*? But *HOW*?
ELOMIRE.

You ... handle the narration;
We'll help you to perform each situation.
(The Prince and troupe assent; Valere, grudgingly and helplessly, gives in and turns to the Prince.)
VALERE.
Then they should be advised, Lord, if I may,
That it is done in verse, this hallowed play ...
PRINCE. *(To the troupe, to impress.)*
In *RHYMING* verse ...
VALERE.

Indeed, it's very odd;
It's almost like ... a miracle of God.
Pentameter, though pleasing on the page
(He does this line metronomically.)
Is SO monOTonOUS upON the STAGE ...
But in *my* hands the opposite is true.
I'm not the one who says that — *others* do!
(Hushing everyone.)
BUT NOW: I dedicate tonight's performance
(Bowing to the Prince.)
To thy most ... MAGNA-GRANDIFIED ENORMANCE!
THE PARABLE OF TWO BOYS FROM CADIZ
(The Parable: It may be performed in a variety of styles, from the most absurdly high to the most outrageously low — in short, anything goes. Valere must cajole, flatter, register pain and ecstasy, blow kisses as he signals various members of the Troupe, like puppets, to assume assorted roles. He is the "Author/Director/Actor/Critic" using all manner of stagecraft and razzle-dazzle.)

THE PARABLE OF TWO BOYS FROM CADIZ
COMMENCES WITH A CHILD NAMED ESMEROLTA
*(Valere places a girl's wig on Bejart's head and leads him forward;
Bejart endures this, slightly humiliated.)*
THE MOST REVOLTING GIRL IN ALL OF VOLTA!
GROWN MEN WHO GLANCED AT HER WOULD RUN
    AND HIDE
(He directs Du Parc and De Brie to act this out.)
FOR WHILE THE LASS WAS BEAUTIFUL INSIDE
WITHOUT FAIR LOOKS SHE DIDN'T STAND A
    CHANCE
IN VOLTA'S VAIN SOCIETY ...
(He tiptoes up to the Prince; with a wink.)
                         ... (Read FRANCE!)
ELOMIRE.
Read France! My God! What's this? A commentary?
VALERE.
I'm merely pointing out that there's a very
Illuminating parallel between
Contemporary France and what we've seen
To be the case in Volta! Why the tension?
PRINCE.
I think it adds an interesting dimension.
Go on, Valere!
VALERE.
              As Lord commands, I do:
(He sneers at Elomire, then continues.)
CONSTRAINED TO KEEP HER VISAGE OUT OF VIEW
A MAIDEN AS GROTESQUE AS ESMEROLTA
STOOD LITTLE OPPORTUNITY IN VOLTA
EXCEPT TO JOIN A SIDESHOW, WHICH SHE DID.
(He hangs a frame around Bejart's head.)
NOW, IF THERE WAS A CROWNING TRICK AMID
THE SEVERAL SHE DEVELOPED, IT WAS WHEN
SHE'D CLAMP HER TEETH AROUND A CLUCKING
    HEN

AND SQUEEZE THE EGGS OUT SLOWLY, ONE BY
    ONE!

(He forces Bejart to do this.)

AND THEN, BY WAY OF ROUNDING OUT THE FUN,
FROM EVERY EGG SHE'D BLOW THE RAW
    ALBUMEN –

(Bejart is forced to do so, and the troupe screams in disgust.)

AN ACT WHICH MADE HER SEEM MORE ... FOWL
    THAN HUMAN!

(Du Parc laughs, and then is quickly ashamed.)

AS ESMEROLTA'S REPUTATION GREW,
THE CROWDS OF GAWKING SPECTATORS DID, TOO.

(He directs the troupe to act accordingly.)

BY MULTITUDES, BY LEGIONS, BY THE SCORE,
BY BOATLOADS THEY ARRIVED FROM EVERY SHORE;
BUT NONE HAD TRAVELLED FARTHER NOR COME
    SOONER
THAN TWO YOUNG FELLOWS IN A PRIVATE
    SCHOONER

(And Valere chooses Elomire and De Brie, who step forward resign-edly.)

WITH "TIT-FOR-TAT" EMBLAZONED ON THE PROW.
MYSTERIOUS THESE BROTHERS WERE! AND HOW!
FRATERNAL TWINS, AND BOTH NAMED ESTEBAN!
DESPITE THAT CURIOUS PHENOMENON
LESS LIKELY TWINS THERE NEVER, EVER WERE:
ONE JUGGLED,

(Valere hands De Brie some juggling balls and De Brie begins to juggle.)

          ONE WAS A PHILOSPHER!

(He slips a tome into Elomire's hands.)

ONE WORE A CAPE, THE OTHER WORE A FROCK;
ONE BOY WAS BIG AND SOLID AS A ROCK,
THE OTHER LOST HIS LEG IN EARLY LIFE
FOR PROVING WRONG A BULLY WITH A KNIFE.

(The troupe encircles Elomire; Valere lets out a banshee cry and "cuts off" Elomire's "leg" – a little wooden boot which he shows to the Prince. As an aside.)

Unless your brain is smaller than a thimble,
The missing leg has struck you as a symbol
For just how very costly it can be
To fight for truth with one's philosophy!
But SOFT! We TARRY! Back to our oration:
THE JUGGLING TWIN, THOUGH SKILLED AT HIS
    VOCATION,
WAS, NONETHELESS, A WEE BIT *ORDINAIRE:*
BEYOND HIS KEEPING THREE BALLS IN THE AIR
THERE WASN'T VERY MUCH THAT HE COULD DO;
(De Brie juggles, incompetently.)
HIS BROTHER, THOUGH, WAS BRILLIANT THROUGH
    AND THROUGH ...
SO BRILLIANT THAT HIS THOUGHTS WERE FAR
    TOO GREAT
FOR ORDINARY FOLK TO CONTEMPLATE!
COMPLEX AND SUBTLE THEOREMS HE'D EXPOUND
(Valère slides a spool of paper into Elomire's mouth and draws it out across the stage, the troupe bunching to read the "theorems.")
OF WHICH THE MOST AGGRESSIVELY PROFOUND
WAS ONE THAT PROVED (AND THIS IS JUST THE
    GIST)
CATHERINE.   *(Reading.)*
THAT NO SUCH THING AS NOTHING CAN EXIST ...
MARQUISE-THERESE.   *(Giggling.)*
FOR IF IT *DOES*, IT CAN'T BE NOTHING, CAN IT?
VALERE.
AMAZING HOW ONE THOUGHT CAN SHAKE THE
    PLANET!
(The whole troupe giggles; with the exception of Bejart and Elomire, they're really beginning to enjoy themselves.)
FOR THIS DISPROOF OF "NOTHING," SHARPLY PUT,
  THE WORLD ... AT LEAST CADIZ ... WAS AT HIS ...
(He holds up the little wooden boot.)
               ... FOOT.

(The troupe laughs spontaneously; they're having fun, and from this point forward they instinctively assume appropriate roles, their pleasure and enthusiasm building in an accelerando.)

IN VOLTA, THOUGH, HE COULDN'T FIND *ONE* FAN!
(The members of the troupe act out the following characters.)
FROM SAGE ARISTOCRAT TO WORKING MAN,
FROM OLDEST VILLAGE COOT TO TINY SHAVER,
THE BROTHER WHOM THE VOLTANS SEEMED TO
    FAVOR
WAS ESTEBAN THE SECOND-RATE MAGICIAN
(De Brie, incompetently, pulls a magic bouquet of flowers from his trousers.)
NOT ESTEBAN THE DAZZLING LOGICIAN;
THE LATTER'S WORK THEY COULDN'T
    UNDERSTAND –
HIS PROOF THAT NOTHING'S NOTHING WAS TOO
    GRAND,
TOO ELOQUENT A THEORY TO ADVANCE
IN SUCH A VAIN AND SHALLOW LAND ...

PRINCE.

                              Read FRANCE.

ELOMIRE.   *(Through clenched teeth.)*
I LOVE that ...

PRINCE.

                Shhhh! It's almost over now.

VALERE.
BUT EVEN MORE UNSETTLING WAS HOW
UNFLINCHINGLY AND SWIFTLY ESMEROLTA,
HERSELF DEBASED BY PREJUDICE IN VOLTA,
GAVE PARTIAL TREATMENT TO THE JUGGLING
    TWIN!
A TOTALLY UNPARDONABLE SIN,
FOR SHE,
(Indicating Bejart.)
           UNLIKE HER COUNTRYMEN, COULD SEE
(Indicating Elomire.)
THE BRILLIANCE OF THE ONE'S PHILOSOPHY
BUT LIKE *THEM*
(And the troupe and Bejart turn toward De Brie.)
           CHOSE THE OTHER ANYWAY!

NOW WHY ON EARTH WOULD SHE BEHAVE THAT
    WAY?
(He draws a tiny mole on Bejart's cheek.)
  IN VOLTA, WHERE A TINY MOLE COULD MAKE
  A CRUCIAL DIFFERENCE TO ONE'S SOCIAL STANDING
(He turns Bejart in the direction of Elomire and shakes him.)
  SHE SHUDDERED AT THE MEREST THOUGHT OF
    BANDING
  WITH SOMEONE SO COMMITTED TO IDEALS
  HE'D SACRIFICE HIS LEG FOR WHAT HE FEELS!
  SHE THEREFORE TOLD THE GENIUS TO MOVE ON ...
  WAS WED TO
*(He pushes Bejart and De Brie together in the frame, throwing rice
over their heads.)*
             MEDIOCRE ESTEBAN ...
  SAID FOND FAREWELLS TO SIDESHOWS AND ALL
    THAT,
  EMBARKED FOR SPAIN ABOARD THE TIT-FOR-TAT
(De Brie steers an imaginary gondola.)
  WHICH SHE MISREAD INSTEAD AS TIT-FOR-TATRA
(He shrugs as if to say "who knows why?")
  WAS WELCOMED TO CADIZ LIKE ... CLEOPATRA
(He winks at the Prince, to celebrate the cleverness of his rhyme.)
DE BRIE.
  "RUFT LAUT MEIN HERTZ!"
CATHERINE.
             BRAVA!
MARQUISE-THERESE.
           WELL GOOD FOR HER!
VALERE.
  BUT ... WHAT OF OUR ESTEEMED PHILOSOPHER?
*(It's clear at this point that there's a real rapport between Valere and
the troupe; and Valere now shoves Elomire aside, himself assuming the
role of "philosopher" for the dramatic finale, as if Elomire couldn't
possibly handle it.)*
MADELEINE.
  ALAS, HIS WAS A HIDEOUS DEMISE!

DU PARC.

BY HUNGER FORCED TO PLUCK OUT BOTH HIS EYES
(Valere "plucks out" two gelatinous "eyes" and hurls them against the wall, where they stick; he then staggers tragically about the stage.)

AND TRADE THEM FOR A SLIGHTLY TAINTED QUAIL
CATHERINE.

HE WANDERED, BLIND AND DESTITUTE AND FRAIL,
DE BRIE.

FROM UPPER VOLTA DOWN TO LOWER VOLTA
DU PARC.

FROM LOWER VOLTA BACK TO UPPER VOLTA
MADELEINE.

IN SEARCH OF SOMEONE
CATHERINE.

              ANYONE AT ALL
MADELEINE.

INTELLIGENT ENOUGH TO SCALE THE WALL
OF HIS COMPLEX AND RICH PHILOSOPHY!
MARQUISE-THERESE.

BUT NOTHING DOES EXIST, FOR TRAGICALLY
  'TWAS NOTHING THAT WAS LEFT UPON THE
    GROUND
  WEEKS LATER WHEN HIS LONELY CORPSE WAS
    FOUND
MADELEINE.

EXCEPT, OF COURSE, THE PATCHES FOR HIS EYES
  AND ALSO
VALERE.

       (Think what this might symbolize!)
MADELEINE.

HIS WOODEN LEG!
VALERE.

       The wooden LEG, YOU HEAR!?
DE BRIE.

THE LEG, LIKE ...
CATHERINE.

     ... TRUTH!

VALERE.

                    Good!

DE BRIE.

                              WOULDN'T DISAPPEAR!
  IT STOOD FOR HIS CONVICTIONS, IN A WAY –
DU PARC.
    UNYIELDING,
MARQUISE-THERESE.

                    HARD,
CATHERINE.

                    IMMUNE TO ALL DECAY,
DE BRIE.
  A MARK OF WHAT HE'D FOUGHT FOR SINCE HIS
        YOUTH:
DU PARC.
    ETERNAL,
MADELEINE.

            IF IMPENETRABLE
ALL.

                    TRUTH!!

(The troupe breaks out into spontaneous applause. Surprised delight,
and mutual admiration for one another's performances. The Prince re-
mains impassive, simply observing.)

VALERE.   *(Shyly covering his face at the applause.)*
  You're kind! You're kind! You're really far too kind!
  O this is so embarrassing I find.
  It's you, not I, who warrant thunderous cheers!
  Applaud yourselves! You've earned the right, my dears:
  Such talent truly takes the breath away –
  You've made the author really *hear* the play
  As though he'd never heard the play before!
  What wizardry is this that makes words ... soar
  That on the page seemed lifeless and mundane ...
DE BRIE.
  Well, acting's very tricky to explain.
  You see, I take the character and try
  To understand not simply *how* but *WHY*

He does the things he does, which is to say
I get *INSIDE* the meaning of the play ...
(De Brie continues babbling as Marquise-Therese steps in front of him.)
MARQUISE-THERESE.
That's nonsense. One must work from outside in:
By putting on the costume I begin
At once to grasp the essence of the part ...
(Marquise-Therese joins De Brie in the babble as Du Parc steps in front of them.)
DU PARC.
It's ludicrous to verbalize my art,
For truly I *BECOME* the words I say!
That chicken – when it's squeezed within your play –
I *WAS* that chicken, I *BECAME* that hen ...
(And Du Parc joins the babble; Catherine steps forward.)
CATHERINE.
It's really *timing:* always knowing *when*
To tilt your head or launch a comic line;
A skill which only TRAINING can refine ...
(And Catherine joins the babble; Madeleine steps forward.)
MADELEINE.
Well – I'm not one who thinks or broods or whines:
I simply hit my mark and say my lines ...
(The Prince rises suddenly to speak; his words are cold and analytically unfriendly: Is he being extremely rigorous and serious about a work which he admires, or has he been so offended that he is preparing to cut off Valere's head?)
PRINCE.
Although the tale's essentially the same
As that which I remember having heard,
Until tonight I thought its themes referred
To Volta only, not some great expanse:
But now I see that Volta is like France ...
VALERE.   *(Wary; trying to make the best of a nervous situation.)*
  Well grasped, my lord!

PRINCE.

                    ... and France like Volta is!
  The Parable of Two Boys from Cadiz
  Critiques, therefore, at least implicitly,
  The foibles of our *own* society!
VALERE.

  But is my work *that* subtle and ambitious!!??
PRINCE.

  I consequently found it more ... *pernicious* ...
  Than when I heard it in the public square!
  For what you're really saying here, Valere,
  (Unless I'm analyzing it too much)
  Is that, like Volta's culture, *ours* is such
  Where mediocrity is bound to thrive
  While excellence must struggle to survive!
VALERE.   *(Really beginning to sweat.)*

  Exactly as you say! It's *very* sad!
PRINCE.

  We punish virtue; we reward the bad;
  Our age embraces dullness like a lover!
*(The members of the troupe begin to fan themselves and look dis-
tracted, not sure which way this is going to fall. They assume a pos-
ture that says, "We're just actors." The Prince slowly, gravely, creep-
ily.)*

  We've lost the taste and patience to discover
  Real morals or real wisdom or real art:
  We can't tell truth and travesty apart!
  And those who can, as shown by Esmerolta,
  Are prone in France, the way they are in Volta,
  To sell their souls without a second thought
  The second there's occasion to be bought!
(Into Valere's ear, almost whispered.)

  Vain fools control the world, *that's* what you're saying!
(Valere is stock-still, and in panic.)

  Because of them our standards are decaying!
  But wiser men must bear the greater blame
  Who tolerate this evil in the name

Of comfort for themselves, like Esmerolta!

Indeed, not France, but all the world, is Volta!

VALERE.   *(Panic.)*

Repeat that final sentence if you could!

An artist rarely feels so *understood!*

(Closing his eyes to enjoy it as he would a haunting melody.)

Just one more time ...

PRINCE.   *(Eerily.)*

                              "Indeed, not France ..."

VALERE.   *(Butting in to finish it himself.)*

                                        LET ME!

(Saying it slowly, savoringly.)

"But all the world is Volta!"

(Gasps again.)

                         Ecstasy!

Had thou, Lord, not been born of regal stripe,

Thou would'st have been a literary type –

A critic, I'm convinced, of world renown!

(Drawing a piece of paper out of his doublet.)

In fact, I'd like to write that sentence down.

I mean – my God! – it really was a dandy!

Who knows when such a line might come in handy?

(Pen poised.)

Again please, Mister Critic? "France, not Volta ... "

PRINCE.   *(Very eerily.)*

"Indeed, not France, but all the world, is Volta!"

(The members of the troupe pull away, fearful, cringing. Valere gulps, then writes down the Prince's words, nervously speaking them in the same eerie tone as he does so.)

VALERE.

"Indeed, not France, but all the world, is Volta!"

(Holding the page at a distance from his face, and reading it in a booming voice.)

"INDEED, NOT FRANCE, BUT ALL THE WORLD, IS
        VOLTA!"

(He drops the quill and paper, swallows hard and begins to speak frantically.)

I'm useless as a critic. Yes, it's so!
Creative people often are, you know.
I don't know *why*, but it's a common quirk –
Especially when judging one's own work.
To do so is like ...
(Shielding his eyes.)

               ... staring at the sun ...
But since my lord already has begun
To offer *his* impressions of my play,
For sake of balance here's the author's way
Of getting at the meaning of the tale:
Correctly, Lord, you've shown how I assail
The slipping standards of our shallow culture;
How vice looms over virtue like a vulture;
How truth's devoured by mediocrity!
But what, apparently, you didn't see
(And it's essential to the story's plan)
Is my insistence that a gifted man
Should persevere no matter what the cost!
One's innovative theories may be lost
On pinheads of the drawing room élite –
In time you might be begging on the street,
Obscurely counting mishaps that befell you:
Perfection can be painful, let me tell you!
The road to Greatness is a bumpy road!
But better pauper prince than wealthy toad,
And if one has to beg then beg one *should!*
It's burdensome to have a leg of wood,
It's difficult to be completely pure!
But they're the heroes, those who can endure,
Excel, be true, preserve integrity:
A harder life, but ... look it ... works for *me!*
(Pause.)
Well, there you have *my* reading of the play!
(Looks to the troupe for help.)
I'd love to hear what *you* all have to say!
(But Elomire, who has been leaning against the wall, now steps forward.)

ELOMIRE.   *(Quietly but with great authority.)*
    MY LORD: this may sound insolent, I know,
    But if *we* stay,
(Pointing to Valere.)
                    then *HE* will have to go!
BEJART.   *(Tries to preempt Elomire's ultimatum.)*
    MY LORD!
ELOMIRE.
                The troupe stands by me ...
PRINCE.   *(Hushing Bejart.)*
                                Let him finish...!
ELOMIRE.
    ... Bejart's afraid that frankness might diminish
    Our chances of remaining here at court;
    He errantly presumes that you're the sort
    Who brooks no disagreement with his views,
    And would, were his beliefs contested, choose
    To banish the offending opposition
    Instead of reassessing his position.
    How wrong he is, my lord, how *very* wrong!
    And that's what I've been saying all along:
    The unembroidered TRUTH is what you seek!
    Since no one feels at liberty to speak,
    I therefore feel compelled to speak for *them!*
    In short: I unreservedly condemn
    By every measure, every standard known,
    A work which I believe could stand alone
    Among the theatre's most profound disgraces!
    Evincing neither talent nor its traces,
    The Parable of Two Boys from Cadiz
    Assuredly, indubitably is
    As bad a stage play as I've ever seen –
    It's pompous, it's insulting, it's obscene,
    It should, in sum, be banned from public view ...
VALERE.
    Well, that's a ... *semi*-positive review ...
(Nervous laughter from a few members of the troupe.)

ELOMIRE.
   He says its composition is unique!
   But have you ever heard a worse technique!!??
   Those desperation couplets are too tragic:
   Like Volta/Esmerolta
VALERE.
                          That's pure *magic* ...
ELOMIRE.
   And Cleopatra/tit-for-tatra! Really!
   Good verse conceals its artifice ideally,
   But his bends over backwards for a rhyme!
   The words are warped to fit some paradigm
   As though the form should legislate the meaning;
   And thus, you'll find no content intervening
   Where his poetic metaphors are made!
VALERE.   *(Tugging at Elomire's sleeve, hushing him.)*
   You're giving out the secrets of the trade!
ELOMIRE.
   But *most* appalling is the allegory!
   If I'm correct, that deeply vulgar story
   Was meant to illustrate the proposition
   That France is in so desperate a condition –
   Its values so decayed, its brow so low –
   That mediocrity is all we know!
VALERE.
   Exactly! Yes! Our culture is bereft
   Of excellence – there's nothing *good* that's *left!*
   And even *good* things aren't any good!
(Struck by his own phrase.)
   (Although *that* phrase was really rather *good!!*)
(Guffaw.)
ELOMIRE.
   Did you hear *that!*? Well, *that's* my main objection!
   Decrying France's vulgar predilection
   For cheap and undistinguished works of art,
   His play, ironically, is from the start
   As bad as any work that it decries!
   This bleak phenomenon *itself* implies

A danger to our nation more malign
Than so-called facts of cultural decline!
It represents a far more lethal trend:
The language used by artists to defend
Against the rule of mediocrity
Has been appropriated to a "t"
By just those mediocrities who rule!
It's dangerous to be governed by a fool,
But worse when fools bemoan the sad decline
Of standards which *their* efforts undermine!
To mourn decaying values in a play
Which only reinforces the decay
Devalues the idea that it expresses!
(Indicating Valere.)
And so the themes he loftily addresses –
Real excellence, real wisdom, and real art –
Are each devalued, sundered, torn apart!
Devalued are the very *words* employed
Which keep ideals from being thus destroyed:
A currency, that's cheapened bit by bit
Till even *genuine* seems counterfeit!
Hence, language is, by fools, emasculated!
Because their deeds and words are unrelated,
They taint all discourse with a hollow drivel:
Words, sapped of meaning, lose their clout, and shrivel!
Convictions, truths, are merely cloaks to don,
Providing an excuse to babble on!
On words *themselves* do such false words reflect;
Indeed, instead of having an effect,
They yield more *words* – they yield *interpretations!*
His play, he says, has subtle implications
About a culture doomed to the abyss!
But since his bold and grand analysis
Is more impressive than his puny play,
It shows that what you *really* do or say
Is less important than the *commentary!*
Good art – good deeds – become ... unnecessary:

What's crucial is *portraying* them as good!
Hard facts count less than *how* they're understood;
Pretension and the truth become confused!
The honest Word is *violently* abused;
And when the honest Word is stripped of sense,
Its *form* assumes unnatural consequence:
The *way* a thing is stated holds more weight,
Than what, if anything, one seeks to state!
"I do my play in rhyme," he says with bluff
As if refined expression were enough
To pardon an impoverishment of thought!
Yet that's the place to which we've now been brought:
A place where men, as far as *I* can see,
Aspire to saying nothing ... endlessly!
Well: *let* them talk and talk until they're blue!
For us, the less that's said, the better ...
DORINE.

TRUE!

BEJART.
Hush up, Dorine!
ELOMIRE.

Valere, I *loathed* your play.
If fools control the world and its decay
It is your play itself that tells us why:
For are you not the fool that you decry!?
VALERE.   *(Rising.)*
Is *that a question!?* Jesus *CHRIST* it's long!!
(Nervous laughter from a few members of the troupe.)
Well! Here's a one-word answer, darling:
    WWRROOOONNG!!
(Valere is playing to the troupe now, trying to break the tension.)
No, no. I'm sure you're right. I'm sure you are.
I'm terrible. I'm quite the worst by far!
I'm all the awful things you say I am!
O DAMN ME!
PRINCE.   *(In a quiet rage, almost unheard.)*
            Silence.

VALERE.

                    DAMN ME! DAMN DAMN DAMN!
VALERE.

   If I could get away from me I would ... ⎫
PRINCE.

   I said, be QUIET!   ⎬

PRINCE.   *(Reeling on Valere.)*   ⎭

   SHUT UP, YOU *FOOL!*

(Valere recoils.)

                    NOW IS THAT UNDERSTOOD?!
*(Elomire attempts to speak, but the Prince turns on him with simi-
lar rage.)*

ELOMIRE.
                                                       ⎫
   My lord ...
                                                       ⎬
PRINCE.
                                                       ⎭
   AND *YOU* AS WELL: how *dare* you lecture me
As if I lacked impartiality
To judge this work afresh, as we agreed!
I frankly feel insulted by your screed!

(Deadly.)

   Don't ever – EVER – talk to me that way!

(Slight shift of mood.)

   Still I can hear the truth in what you say;
You know I do. You've had my full support
In voicing all such sentiments at Court,
And though I recognize them and *agree*
They've weighed upon your plays increasingly!
Stand firm for "truth in language" – but be FAIR:
To turn *those* arguments against Valere
(Who has a simple talent that might be
A happy antidote) is SOPHISTRY!
The *truth,* of course, is that you can't allow
That "ELOMIRE HIMSELF" is *wrong,* somehow!

(Indicating the troupe.)

   "He'd ruin us," you said. You're INCORRECT.
In fact I was delighted to detect
A message in his play that made it more
Intriguingly disturbing than before –

(Indicating the troupe again.)
    And it was met with quite a great ovation.
(Turns to Valere; the discussion is ended, the bargain is won.)
    Monsieur Valere: you have an invitation
    To join the troupe; to bring your talents here.
VALERE.
    Who, *me!*? And share the stage with *Elomire!*?
    No, no I couldn't.
(Very slight pause.)
                  Well, if you *insist!*
    Humility doth urge me to resist,
    But *damn* humility I always say!
    Just show me where to sign! I'm here to stay!
    It's really too too generous of you;
    My friends, I'm speechless ...
ELOMIRE.
                Would that *that* were true!
    But I'm convinced that that will *never* be!
    My lord, I said with all sincerity
    That if *we* stay then *he* will have to go:
    That wasn't just an idle threat, you know...!
PRINCE.   *(Deadly serious, even belligerent.)*
    Well, *he's* not going *anywhere,* all right!?
    So you can pack your bags and leave tonight
(Indicating the troupe.)
    And they can join you if they're so inclined;
    And since it comes to that, I think you'll find
    A precious few supporters for this action!
    How sad to let a negative reaction
    To someone whom you've barely even met
    Irrevocably alter and upset
    Your place at Court, your troupe's security!
    And in the name of *what* – of *purity?*
    Of strict adherence to some rigid rule?
    One really has to wonder – who's the fool?
(The question lingers. Pause. He turns to address the troupe.)
    To those who want to leave with Elomire,
    I thank you for your splendid service here

And wish you well whatever you may do;
But, otherwise, as for the rest of you –
The ones without a moral cross to bear
Who might *enjoy* performing with Valere –
We have a thing or two to talk about
And therefore come ... accompany me out!

(Exit Prince and servants. Pause. Elomire turns to the troupe.)

ELOMIRE.
I thought ... I hoped ... that he would understand.
It's not what I ... it isn't what I'd planned.
There simply wasn't any choice, you see?
To ask you ...

(He breaks off, stutters. He is silent for a moment. Emotion seizes him.)

    ... this is difficult for me ...

(Pause. He partially regains himself.)

To ask you ... to give up this life for one
Whose hardships we had only just begun
By mercy to forget ...

(And he is overwhelmed, shocked to find that he is suddenly, for the first time, inarticulate.)

    ... no ... WORDS ... will do.

(Brief pause. Again, he finds words.)

But know: your faith in me and mine in you
Has tided us through troubled times before
And will again. It *WILL*!

(He breaks off again.)

    There's nothing more ...

(He turns U. to get his coat.)

Let's get our things ... I've nothing more to add ...

DE BRIE. *(Steps forward.)*
Excuse me, Elomire ...

(Clears his throat, indicates Valere; sheepishly.)

    ... he's not so bad.

(Elomire turns to face De Brie, who says, with a little more confidence.)

I mean ... I *liked* his play ... a tiny bit.

ELOMIRE.   *(Softly, from far away.)*
    Don't lie.
DE BRIE.
                    I'm sorry. That's the truth of it.
ELOMIRE.   *(Softly, distant.)*
    That *can't* be true ...
CATHERINE.
                        Well don't look so dejected!
    He wasn't the disgrace that we expected.
VALERE.   *(With a hard edge.)*
    Why child. Such honeyed words. Such flattery.
ELOMIRE.   *(Emerging from the distance.)*
    My God. This can't be happening to me.
    Du Parc...!
DU PARC.   *(Genuine.)*
                    I'm sorry, I agree with her.
ELOMIRE.
    Therese...?
MARQUISE-THERESE.
                Me too.
VALERE.   *(Quietly, enjoying this.)*
                    You ... "love me" ... as it were!
ELOMIRE.
    He really took you in, this Boor of boors?
MADELEINE.
    Well, dear ... his work *is* livelier than yours.
ELOMIRE.   *(Shock; it's caving in.)*
    It's WHAT?
MARQUISE-THERESE.
                It's more accessible and fun!
CATHERINE.
    It frankly seems forever since we've done
    A play that might have popular appeal!
DE BRIE.
    Were we to tour again I strongly feel
    That with its showy costumes, gags, and plot
    It's bound to draw great crowds ...

MARQUISE-THERESE.
(With a hint of exasperation, as if Elomire had lost a sense of play in his work and became too didactic, too insensitive to their needs as a troupe.)

As we could not
With all the work of YOURS we've done of late.
Who really cares about the
(As if quoting from one of Elomire's plays.)
bloated state
Of language and its ethical dimension,
And other themes too ponderous to mention
Which tend to bore instead of entertain ...
DU PARC.
It's arrogance that leads you to disdain
A play which could become a great success ...
ELOMIRE.   *(Deeply confused, shaken.)*
And that's what you desire?
DU PARC.

Well ...
ALL.   *(Affectionately, but firmly.)*
Frankly, yes.
VALERE.   *(Again, quietly, off to the side.)*
My dears, you're giving me a swollen head.
ELOMIRE.   *(Dumbfounded.)*
Are you prepared to live with what you've said?
Have you considered what this choice will mean?
Does no one understand?
DORINE.   *(Very quietly, almost unheard.)*
I do.
ELOMIRE.   *(Turns to her; in amazement, as in a dream.)*
Dorine.
BEJART.   *(From the other side of the stage; ambiguously, with what could be either fatalism or reproval.)*
I do as well.
ELOMIRE.   *(Goes to him.)*
Then help me, please, Bejart.
Dear friend, stick with me ...

BEJART.

No. You've gone too far.

ELOMIRE.

I have?

BEJART.

There *is* a way that's less extreme.

ELOMIRE.   *(Retrenching.)*

I don't believe that.

BEJART.   *(Crosses to the door, not looking at Elomire.)*

No, so it would seem.

ELOMIRE.

And *you* don't either.

(Bejart summons the troupe, trying to ignore Elomire; he opens the door.)

BEJART.

Come along, you hear?

ELOMIRE.

I *KNOW* YOU DON'T.

BEJART.   *(Looks at Elomire; clearly.)*

I *have* to, Elomire.

(Pause. To the troupe.)

The Prince is waiting, everyone. Let's go.

(Elomire turns to the troupe.)

ELOMIRE.   *(Finally, beseechingly.)*

Don't leave me.

(But the troupe exits, the door held open by Bejart. A moment passes. To Bejart.)

Please.

(Pause.)

BEJART.

Then stay.

(Pause.)

ELOMIRE.

I can't.

(Pause.)

BEJART.

I know.

(Bejart holds up his hand to Elomire, exits. Elomire crosses up to the closed door and leans against it. Pause. From the other side of the stage, Valere beings to speak, with some real menace, first to the audience, then to Elomire.)

VALERE.

WELL! Talk about a party falling flat!
They all just ... *disappeared!* ... did you see *that!*?
A pity! We were having *lots* of fun!
And I was so *adored* by everyone!!
But not by Elomire, I'm sad to say
Which casts a sort of pall across the day
Since, after all, that's *really* why I'm here!

(To Elomire.)

If only you had *LIKED* me, Elomire:
We had the makings of a brilliant team!
But now it lies there, just a shattered dream,
And all that's left to do is say "goodnight."

(Collecting himself.)

For me, just meeting you was a delight!
I'm sorry that you didn't feel the same,
But thank you, anyway. I'm glad I came.

(He begins to exit.)

Our dinner here I never shall forget ...

(Exit Valere; then, after a beat, he sticks his head back into the room and says.)

... Especially that *DREADFUL* vinaigrette ...

(Elomire winces. Exit Valere. Elomire puts his coat on and the lights dim until he remains in a pin spot only.)

ELOMIRE.   *(This final speech is spoken quietly, to himself.)*

By starting on a journey once again
(Not knowing what's to come, or where I'm bound)
I wonder – did I stand too firmly, then,
When this safe haven had at last been found?

Does any way less radical exist
To keep ideals from being trivialized?
The only way I know is to resist:
Autonomy cannot be compromised!

(Elomire lifts his head to see Dorine, who has never left the stage and is standing in the shadows, listening.)
>With every day the peril is increased
>Of yielding to this treacherous misrule,
>For fools contain inside of them a beast
>That triumphs when the world is made a fool!

(A low murmur of voices and laughter is heard from the other room.)
>If LIFE – not grim survival – is the aim,
>The only hope is setting out to find
>A form of moral discourse to reclaim
>The moral discourse fools have undermined.

>Upon that road I joyfully embark!
>And though it seems that joy itself's at stake,
>There's joy itself in challenging the dark:
>We're measured by the *choices* that we make!

(An eruption of laughter from offstage. Dorine slowly crosses to Elomire, carrying his belongings to him.)
>Against great odds one gamely perseveres,
>For nature gives advantage to a fool:
>His mindless laughter ringing in your ears,
>His thoughtless cruelties seeming doubly cruel;

>His power stems from emptiness and scorn –
>Debasing the ideals of common men;
>But those debased ideals *can* be reborn ...
>By starting on the journey once again.

(Laughter and noise from offstage. Elomire takes his suitcase from Dorine. Pause. He exits. From the other room, we hear Valere's voice boom.)
VALERE.   *(Off.)*
>YOU THINK ME *TOO* SELF-CRITICAL? ALACK,
>TEN THOUSAND MORE HAVE LAUNCHED THE SAME
>   ATTACK!

(The voices dissolve and are replaced by music. Dorine, alone, blows a kiss to Elomire; her eyes welling with tears, she turns to face the audience in silence as the curtain falls.)

END OF PLAY

PROPERTY LIST

1 12-foot staff
1 12-foot pink feather duster
1 piece of parchment paper
1 feather quill
1 water-base black marker
1 printed writ (BEJART)
handkerchief (VALERE)
magic bouquet of flowers
small brown suitcase
gold suitcase with lights
large gold suitcase with:
    picture frame
    shoulder brace
    fireworks detonator
    fake leg
1 set of cymbals
Glitter (VALERE)
Confetti (VALERE)
Paper (VALERE)
Quill (VALERE)
Blond wig (VALERE)
1 rose (VALERE)
3 juggling balls (VALERE)
1 fake chicken with egg, filled with mixture of flour and
    water (for albumen) (VALERE)
Magic paper streamer (to be put in Elomire's mouth (VALERE)
11 fake scripts of "The Parable of Two Boys from Cadiz"
    (VALERE)
Fake eye balls on elastic (VALERE)
1 eyebrow pencil (VALERE)

COSTUME PLOT

ELOMIRE
2 white shirts
White dickey
Black pants
Black coat
Black velvet shoes
3 pair black socks
3 T-shirts
Black suspenders

BEJART
2 white shirts
Green coat
Black pants
Black shoes
3 pair black socks
3 T-shirts
1 hump-back padded suit

VALERE
2 pink shirts
2 tan shirts
Leopard brown pants
Orange pants
Orange/green jacket
Orange/green vest
Brown sandals
Green and pink shoes
3 T-shirts
2 pair green hose
2 pair pink hose

PRINCE CONTI
2 white shirts
Purple coat
Purple vest
Purple breeches
Purple sash
Pink shoes
Pink ring
3 pair pink tights
3 T-shirts
3 dance belts

DE BRIE
2 white shirts
2 white dickeys
Lavender coat
Lavender vest
Lavender pants
Lavender shoes
Stick pin
Rings
3 pair lavender socks
3 T-shirts
3 dance belts

RENE DU PARC
2 white shirts
2 white dickeys
Yellow coat
Yellow vest
Yellow pants
Yellow shoes
3 yellow socks
3 T-shirts

DORINE
Black maid's dress
Black pantaloons
3 pair black tights
3 pair dance trunks
6 black T-shirts
Black shoes

MADELEINE BEJART
Blue dress with bodice
Blue petticoat
Cream kid gloves
1 necklace
1 pair earrings
Black shoes
Hose

CATHERINE DE BRIE
Pink dress with bodice
Pink petticoat
Cream kid gloves
1 necklace
1 pair earrings
1 bracelet
Pink shoes
Hose

MARQUISE THERESE DU PARC
Red dress with bodice
Red petticoat
Cream kid gloves
1 necklace
1 pair earrings
1 bracelet
Red shoes
Hose

SERVANTS
White coat
White pants
3 pair black tights
3 pair white gloves
3 T-shirts
Black padded suit
Black shoes

SOUND EFFECTS

Booming organ sound

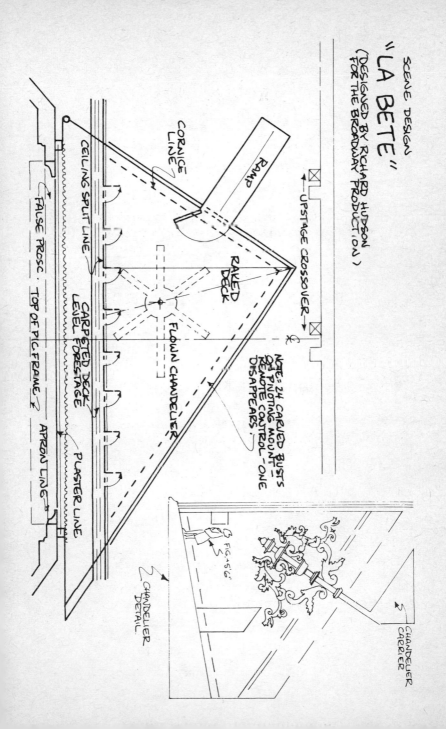

SCENE DESIGN
"LA BÊTE"
(DESIGNED BY RICHARD HUDSON
FOR THE BROADWAY PRODUCTION)

CORNICE LINE

RAMP

← UPSTAGE CROSSOVER →

CEILING SPLIT LINE

RAKED DECK

CARPETED DECK LEVEL FORESTAGE

FLOWN CHANDELIER

NOTE: 24 CARVED BUSTS
ON PIVOTING MOUNT -
REMOTE CONTROL - ONE
DISAPPEARS.

FALSE PROSC. TOP OF PIC FRAME

APRON LINE

PLASTER LINE

FIG - 5 - 6"

CHANDELIER
DETAIL.

CHANDELIER
CARRIER

NEW PLAYS

BEFORE IT HITS HOME
by Cheryl L. West

APPROXIMATING MOTHER
by Kathleen Tolan

THE MANCHURIAN CANDIDATE
by John Lahr

VEINS AND THUMBTACKS
by Jonathan Marc Sherman

BARGAINS
by Jack Heifner

ARTIFICIAL REALITY
by Jeffrey Essmann

Write for information as to availability

DRAMATISTS PLAY SERVICE, INC.
440 Park Avenue South   New York, N.Y. 10016

NEW PLAYS

FOUR BABOONS ADORING THE SUN
by John Guare

**THE KATHY AND MO SHOW:
PARALLEL LIVES**
by Mo Gaffney and Kathy Najimy

RAFT OF THE MEDUSA
by Joe Pintauro

STATES OF SHOCK
by Sam Shepard

MINOR DEMONS
by Bruce Graham

DEARLY DEPARTED
by David Bottrell and Jessie Jones

Write for information as to availability

DRAMATISTS PLAY SERVICE, INC.
440 Park Avenue South   New York, N.Y. 10016

NEW PLAYS

I HATE HAMLET
by Paul Rudnick

THE OLD BOY
by A.R. Gurney

THE FEVER
by Wallace Shawn

DAYTRIPS
by Jo Carson

LA BÊTE
by David Hirson

FORTINBRAS
by Lee Blessing

Write for information as to availability

DRAMATISTS PLAY SERVICE, INC.
440 Park Avenue South   New York, N.Y. 10016